# TRUE COLORS

## An EFL Course for Real Communication

## 1A with Workbook

Jay Maurer

Irene E. Schoenberg

Joan Saslow

Series Director

LONGMAN

**True Colors: An EFL Course for Real Communication
1A with Workbook**

Addison Wesley Longman, 10 Bank Street, White Plains, NY 10606

Senior acquisitions editor: Allen Ascher
Director of design and production: Rhea Banker
Managing editor: Linda Moser
Production manager: Alana Zdinak
Production supervisor: Liza Pleva
Production editor: Alda Trabucchi
Senior manufacturing manager: Patrice Fraccio
Cover design: Rhea Banker
Text design: Word & Image Design
Text composition: Word & Image Design
Illustrations: Pierre Berthiaume, Jocelyn Bouchard, Eric Colquhoun,
    Brian Hughes, Don Kilby, Paul McCusker, Dusan Petricic,
    Quack Communications, Stephen Quinlan, Richard Row,
    Steve Shulman, Teco, Margot Thompson, Angela Vaculik
Photography: Gilbert Duclos

ISBN 0-201-60376-4

1 2 3 4 5 6 7 8 9 10—CRK—03 02 01 00 99 98

# Contents

# Scope and Sequence of Specific Content and Skills for 1A and 1B

| UNIT | Social Language | Vocabulary | Grammar | Listening |
|------|-----------------|------------|---------|-----------|
| **1 Are you in this class?** <br> page 2 | How to: <br> • make informal introductions <br> • talk about occupations <br> • ask questions / make negative statements <br> • describe people | • nouns for talking about people <br> • occupations <br> • nouns and adjectives that describe people | • verb *be*--use and form <br> • subject pronouns <br> • contractions <br> • indefinite and definite articles | Type: <br> • a TV quiz program <br> Comprehension Skill: <br> • focus attention |
| **2 There's a noise downstairs!** <br> page 14 | How to: <br> • say the time <br> • identify yourself on the phone / ask how someone is <br> • make plans to meet <br> • describe things and places | • telling time <br> • prepositions for times of the day and dates | • count and non-count nouns: *there is/there are* | Types: <br> • a recorded announcement <br> • a phone conversation <br> Comprehension Skills: <br> • focus attention <br> • determine context |
| **3 For computer questions, press one now.** <br> page 26 | How to: <br> • suggest an activity/an alternative <br> • state address / phone number <br> • describe family relationships | • social activities <br> • machines and appliances <br> • family relationships <br> • classroom commands | • commands <br> • suggestions with *let's* <br> • possessive adjectives <br> • possessive nouns | Type: <br> • a voice mail message <br> Comprehension Skill: <br> • focus attention |
| **4 What's Bob doing?** <br> page 38 | How to: <br> • talk about actions in progress <br> • apologize <br> • offer to call back later <br> • give directions to a place <br> • talk about order | • everyday activities <br> • ordinal numbers <br> • locations and directions | • the present continuous <br> • object pronouns | Type: <br> • a phone conversation <br> Comprehension Skill: <br> • determine context |
| **5 You lose it. We find it.** <br> page 50 | How to: <br> • talk about work <br> • ask about and express likes <br> • talk about studies <br> • express dislikes <br> • talk about habitual activities | • places to work <br> • fields of study <br> • adjectives to describe studies | • the simple present tense | Types: <br> • a photo story <br> • a story about detectives <br> • a conversation in an office <br> Comprehension Skills: <br> • confirming content <br> • determine context <br> • focus attention |
| **Review of Units 1–5** <br> page 62 | | | | |
| **6 We're going to win.** <br> page 72 | How to: <br> • make an appointment <br> • talk about pains / illnesses <br> • describe plans <br> • talk about frequency <br> • describe feelings | • parts of the body <br> • general locations <br> • aches, pains, and illnesses <br> • frequency adverbs | • the future with *be going to* <br> • placement of frequency adverbs | Types: <br> • interviews <br> Comprehension Skills: <br> • determine context <br> • focus attention |
| **7 Can you dance?** <br> page 84 | How to: <br> • express obligations / regrets <br> • make invitations with *let's* <br> • ask for help <br> • express gratitude <br> • talk about ability | • leisure activities <br> • academic subjects | • *have to / has to* <br> • *can* | Types: <br> • conversations <br> Comprehension Skills: <br> • determine context <br> • focus attention |
| **8 Do you want some pizza, Lulu?** <br> page 96 | How to: <br> • get someone's attention <br> • ask about price <br> • agree to buy <br> • state a need <br> • express disbelief | • clothing <br> • colors | • *some* and *any* <br> • *one* and *ones* <br> • *this, that, these,* and *those* | Types: <br> • a story about a boy's life <br> • a conversation <br> Comprehension Skills: <br> • factual recall <br> • focus attention |
| **9 Weren't you at Alice's?** <br> page 108 | How to: <br> • talk about the past <br> • give and accept an apology <br> • confirm identity <br> • talk about ownership and possession | • past time expressions <br> • social and business relationships | • the past tense of *be* <br> • possessive pronouns | Type: <br> • a telephone conversation <br> Comprehension Skills: <br> • focus attention |
| **10 My plane just landed.** <br> page 120 | How to: <br> • talk about past actions and facts <br> • talk about recent activities <br> • empathize | • more past time expressions | • the simple past tense of regular and irregular verbs | Type <br> • an extended dialogue <br> Comprehension Skill: <br> • determine context |
| **Review of Units 6–10** <br> page 132 | | | | |

iv

| Reading | Writing | Pronunciation | Expression of Opinions |
|---|---|---|---|
| Types:<br>• a photo story<br>• a newspaper article<br>Comprehension Skills:<br>• confirming content<br>• factual recall | Task:<br>• addressing an envelope<br>Skill:<br>• capitalization of names of people and places | • the alphabet | • opinions of occupations and studies |
| Types:<br>• a photo story<br>• short paragraphs<br>Comprehension Skills:<br>• factual recall<br>• identifying the main idea | Task:<br>• a short note to a classmate<br>Skill<br>• period and question mark | • /s/, /z/, and /iz/ | • favorite places |
| Types:<br>• a photo story<br>• advertisements<br>Comprehension Skills:<br>• confirming content<br>• factual recall | Type:<br>• phone messages<br>Skill:<br>• writing names, times, and phone numbers | • stress and meaning | • value of certain machines and appliances |
| Types:<br>• a photo story<br>• an extended dialogue<br>Comprehension Skills:<br>• confirming content<br>• drawing conclusions | Type:<br>• a letter<br>Skill:<br>• spelling present participles | • /iʸ/ and /i/ | • opinions about lateness |
| Type:<br>• an extended dialogue<br>Comprehension Skills:<br>• identifying the main idea | Type:<br>• note taking<br>Skill:<br>• writing the simple present tense | • /s/, /z/, and /iz/ | • tastes in foods, people, music, etc. |
| Types:<br>• a photo story<br>• an extended dialogue<br>Comprehension Skills:<br>• drawing conclusions<br>• interpretation and analysis | Type:<br>• a business letter<br>Skill:<br>• a formal letter style | • intonation of questions | • good and bad ways to meet people<br>• opinions about meeting and dating |
| Types:<br>• a photo story<br>• an essay<br>Comprehension Skills:<br>• confirming content<br>• factual recall | Type:<br>• a student newspaper article<br>Skill:<br>• developing paragraphs | • *can* and *can't* in sentences (stressed and unstressed) | • reasons why people like or dislike dancing |
| Type:<br>• an extended dialogue<br>Comprehension Skill:<br>• interpretation and analysis | Type:<br>• an extended dialogue<br>Skills:<br>• use of colon in dialogue style<br>• writing questions in the simple present tense and the present continuous | • /ɑ/ and /ʌ/ | • problems between parents and children<br>• how can families communicate better? |
| Types:<br>• a photo story<br>• an extended dialogue<br>Comprehension Skills:<br>• confirming content<br>• understanding meaning from context | Type:<br>• a paragraph about dating<br>Skill:<br>• development of a topic sentence | • the /r/ and /h/ sounds<br>• the /r/ and /l/ sounds<br>• the /r/, /d/ , and /t/ sounds | • who pays on a date? |
| Types:<br>• a photo story<br>• a magazine article<br>Comprehension Skills:<br>• factual recall<br>• understanding meaning from context | Type:<br>• a description of a person<br>Skill:<br>• writing facts about the past | • past tense endings: *worked / played / repeated* | • environment vs. heredity |

# Acknowledgments

••••••••••••••••••••••••••••••••

The authors and series director wish to acknowledge with gratitude the following consultants, reviewers, and piloters—our partners in the development of *True Colors*.

## Consultants

**Berta de Llano**, Puebla, Mexico • **Luis Fernando Gómez J.**, School of Education, University of Antioquia, Colombia • **Irma K. Ghosn**, Lebanese American University, Byblos, Lebanon • **Annie Hu**, Fu-Jen Catholic University, Taipei, Taiwan • **Nancy Lake**, CEL-LEP, São Paulo, Brazil • **Frank Lambert**, Pagoda Foreign Language Institute, Seoul, Korea • **Kazuhiko Yoshida**, Kobe University, Kobe City, Japan.

## Reviewers and Piloters

• **Lucia Adrian**, EF Language Schools, Miami, Florida, USA • **Ronald Aviles**, Instituto Chileno Norteamericano, Chuquicamata, Chile • **Liliana Baltra**, Instituto Chileno Norteamericano, Santiago, Chile • **Paulo Roberto Berkelmans**, CEL-LEP, São Paulo, Brazil • **Luis Beze**, Casa Thomas Jefferson, Brasília, Brazil • **Martin T. Bickerstaff**, ELS Language Centers, Oakland, California, USA • **Mary C. Black**, Institute of North American Studies, Barcelona, Spain • **James Boyd**, ECC Foreign Language Institute, Osaka, Japan • **Susan Bryan de Martínez**, Instituto Mexicano Norteamericano, Monterrey, Mexico • **Hugo A. Buitano**, Instituto Chileno Norteamericano, Arica, Chile • **Gary Butzbach**, American Language Center, Rabat, Morocco • **Herlinda Canto**, Universidad Popular Autónoma del Estado de Puebla, Mexico • **Rigoberto Castillo**, Colegio de CAFAM, Santafé de Bogotá, Colombia • **Tina M. Castillo**, Santafé de Bogotá, Colombia • **Amparo Clavijo Olarte**, Universidad Distrital, Santafé de Bogotá, Colombia • **Graciela Conocente**, Asociación Mendocina de Intercambio Cultural Argentino Norteamerica, Argentina • **Greg Conquest**, Yokohama Gaigo Business College, Japan • **Eduardo Corbo**, IETI, Salto, Uruguay • **Marilia Costa**, Instituto Brasil-Estados Unidos, Rio de Janeiro, Brazil • **Miles Craven**, Nihon University, Shizuoka, Japan • **Michael Davidson**, EF Language Schools, Miami, Florida, USA • **Celia de Juan**, UNICO, UAG, Guadalajara, Mexico • **Laura de Marín**, Centro Colombo Americano, Medellín, Colombia • **Montserrat Muntaner Djmal**, Instituto Brasil-Estados Unidos, Rio de Janeiro, Brazil • **Deborah Donnelley de García**, ITESM-Campus Querétaro, Mexico • **Rosa Erlichman**, União Cultural, São Paulo, Brazil • **Patricia Escalante Arauz**, Universidad de Costa Rica, San Pedro de Montes de Oca, Costa Rica • **Guadalupe Espinoza**, ITESM-Campus Querétaro, Mexico • **Suad Farkouh**, ESL Consultant to Philadelphia National Schools, Amman, Jordan • **Niura R.H. Ferreria**, Centro Cultural Brasil Estados Unidos, Guarapuava, Brazil • **Fernando Fleurquin**, Alianza Cultural Uruguay-EEUU, Montevideo, Uruguay • **Patricia Fleury**, Casa Thomas Jefferson, Brasília, Brazil • **Patricia Foncea**, Colegio Jesualdo, Santiago, Chile • **Areta Ulhana Galat**, Centro Cultural Brasil Estados Unidos, Curitiba, Brazil• **Christina Gitsaki**, Nagoya University of Commerce and Business Administration, Japan • **Julie Harris de Peyré**, Universidad del Valle, Guatemala • **Ruth Hassell de Hernández**, UANL, Mexico • **Mia Kim**, Kyung Hee University, Seoul, Korea • **John Hawkes**, EF International School, Santa Barbara, California, USA •

**Rose M. Hernández**, University of Puerto Rico-Bayamón, Puerto Rico • **Susan Hills**, EF International School of English, San Diego, California, USA • **Jan Kelley**, EF International School, Santa Barbara, California, USA • **Junko Kobayashi**, Sankei International College, Tokyo, Japan • **Gil Lancaster**, Academy Istanbul, Istanbul, Turkey • **Mónica Lobo**, Santiago, Chile • **Luz Adriana Lopera**, Centro Colombo Americano, Medellín, Colombia • **Eva Irene Loya**, ITESM-Campus Querétaro, Mexico • **Mary Maloy Lara**, Instituto John F. Kennedy, Tehuacán, Mexico • **Meire de Jesus Marion**, Associação Alumni, São Paulo, Brazil • **Juliet Marlier**, Universidad de las Américas, Puebla, Mexico • **Yolanda Martínez**, Instituto D'Amicis, Puebla, Mexico • **Neil McClelland**, Shimonoseki City University, Japan • **Regina Celia Pereira Mendes**, Instituto Brasil-Estados Unidos, Rio de Janeiro, Brazil • **Jim Miller**, Yokohama Gaigo Business College, Japan • **Fiona Montarry**, The American Language Center, Casablanca, Morocco • **Luiz Claudio Monteiro**, Casa Thomas Jefferson, Brasília, Brazil • **Angelita Oliveira Moreno**, ICBEU, Belo Horizonte, Brazil • **Ahmed Mohammad Motala**, King Fahd University of Petroleum & Minerals, Dhahran, Saudi Arabia • **William Richard Munzer**, Universidad IDEAS de Bogotá, Colombia • **Akiko Nakazawa**, Yokohama Gaigo Business College, Japan • **Adrian Nunn**, EF International School of English, Los Angeles, California, USA • **Margarita Ordaz Mejía**, Universidad Americana de Acapulco, Mexico • **Sherry Ou**, Fu-Jen Catholic Univ, Taipei, Taiwan • **Thelma Jonas Péres**, Casa Thomas Jefferson, Brasília, Brazil • **Renata Philippov**, Associação Alumni, São Paulo, Brazil • **Ciaran Quinn**, Otemae College, Osaka, Japan • **Ron Ragsdale**, Bilgi University, Istanbul, Turkey • **Luis Ramírez F.**, Instituto Norteamericano de Cultura, Concepción, Chile • **Martha Restrepo Rodríguez**, Politécnico Grancolombiano, Santafé de Bogotá, Colombia • **Irene Reyes Giordanelli**, Centro Cultural Colombo Americano, Santiago de Cali, Colombia • **Dolores Rodríguez**, CELE (Centro de Lenguas), Universidad Autónoma de Puebla, Mexico • **Idia Rodríguez**, University of Puerto Rico-Arecibo, Puerto Rico • **Eddy Rojas & teachers**, Centro de Idiomas de la P. Universidad Católica, Peru • **Ricardo Romero**, Centro Cultural Colombo Americano, Santafé de Bogotá, Colombia • **Blanca Lilia Rosales Bremont**, Universidad Americana de Acapulco, Mexico • **Marie Adele Ryan**, Associação Alumni, São Paulo, Brazil • **Nadia Sarkis**, Uniao Cultural, São Paulo, Brazil • **Andrea Seidel**, Universidad Americana de Acapulco, Mexico • **Hada Shammar**, American Language Center, Amman, Jordan • **Lai Yin Shem**, Centro Colombo Americano, Medellín, Colombia • **Maria Cristina Siqueira**, CEL-LEP, São Paulo, Brazil • **María Inés Sandoval Astudillo**, Instituto Chileno Norteamericano, Chillán, Chile • **Lilian Munhoz Soares**, Centro Cultural Brasil Estados Unidos, Santos, Brazil • **Mário César de Sousa**, Instituto Brasil-Estados Unidos, Fortaleza, Brazil • **Tatiana Suárez**, Politécnico Grancolombiano, Santafé de Bogotá, Colombia • **Richard Paul Taylor**, Nagoya University of Commerce and Business Administration, Japan • **David Thompson**, Instituto Mexicano Norteamericano de Relaciones Culturales, Guadalajara, Mexico • **Mr. Uzawa**, Sankei International College, Tokyo, Japan • **Nilda Valdez**, Centro Cultural Salvadoreño, El Salvador • **Euclides Valencia Cepeda**, Universidad Distrital, Santafé de Bogotá, Colombia • **Ana Verde**, American Language Institute, Montevideo, Uruguay • **Andrea Zaidenberg**, Step English Language Center, Argentina

# Preface

● ● ● ● ● ● ● ● ● ● ● ● ● ● ● ● ● ● ● ● ● ● ● ● ● ● ● ● ● ● ● ● ● ● ● ● ● ● ● ● ● ● ● ● ● ● ●

*True Colors* is a complete and articulated five-level adult or young adult course in English as a foreign language. Each book is intended to be completed in a period of 60 to 90 class hours. There are two possible beginning-level entry points: Basic level or Book 1.

There are two reasons why this course is entitled *True Colors*. It presents the true voice of the native speaker of American English, and it systematically teaches students to communicate *in their own words*—to **let their true colors shine through.**

## Focus and Approach

*True Colors* is a highly communicative international course enhanced by strong four-skills support, including a two-step listening strand and an abundance of games, info-gaps, and other interactive activities. Within each unit short, integrated social language and grammar lessons ensure concentrated oral practice and production. *True Colors* takes into account different learning and teaching styles. It is centered on task-based strategies and the well-known fact that practice in each skill area enhances mastery of the others.

A major innovation of the *True Colors* series is to systematically build students' ability to present their own ideas, opinions, and feelings—both accurately and confidently. For this reason, every activity leads students to gain ownership of the language, progressively moving them *away* from models

to express thoughts in their own words and to improvise based on what they know.

*True Colors* carefully distinguishes between receptive and productive language. It consistently presents language in the receptive mode before—and at a slightly higher difficulty level than—the productive mode. Research has shown that students are more successful when they become familiar with new language before having to produce it. For this reason, *True Colors* presents EFL students with a wealth of both receptive and productive models, combining exposure and practice for increased understanding and attainable mastery.

*True Colors* is specifically designed for use by students who rarely encounter English outside of class. The course is built around a wealth of speaking and reading models of the true voice of the American speaker. This refreshing change from "textbook English" is essential for students who have limited access to real native speech and writing.

Because international students do not have the opportunity to speak to native speakers on a regular basis, *True Colors* does not present activities such as interviewing native speakers or watching TV in English. Instead, the course serves as a replacement for immersion in an English-speaking environment, making the classroom itself a microcosm of the English-speaking world. The goal and promise of *True Colors* is to prepare students to move out of this textbook and to understand, speak, read, and write in the real world.

## Student Population

Book 1 of *True Colors* is written for adult and young adult false beginners. It has been pilot-tested in classrooms throughout the world and with students of numerous language groups.

Book 4 concludes at a high-intermediate level. The Basic level text is an alternative entry point for very weak false beginners or true beginners.

## Course Length

The *True Colors* Student's Books are designed to cover from 60 to 90 class hours of instruction. Although each Student's Book is a complete course in itself, giving presentation, practice, and production of all four skills, a full complement of supplementary materials is available to further expand the material.

## Components of the Course

**Student's Book**   The student's book is made up of ten units and two review units, one coming after unit five and another coming after unit ten.

**Teacher's Edition**   The teacher's edition is interviewed with full-color student's book pages and contains an introduction to the format and approach of *True Colors;* page-by-page teaching suggestions especially written for the teacher who teaches outside an English-speaking country; tapescripts for the audiocassettes; a complete answer key to the exercises in the student's book, workbook, and achievement tests.

**Teacher's Bonus Pack**   The Teacher's Bonus Pack is a unique set of reproducible hands-on learning-support activities that includes flash cards for large- or small-group vocabulary presentations, pronunciation game cards, duplicating masters that contain photo stories with empty speech balloons for student oral and written improvisation, learner-created grammar notes, and interactive conversation cards for social language reinforcement. The Teacher's Bonus Pack provides suggestions for tailoring *True Colors* to the needs of a variety of settings.

**Workbook**   The workbook contains numerous additional opportunities for written reinforcement of the language taught in the student's book. The exercises in the workbook are suitable for homework or for classwork.

**Audiocassettes**   The audiocassettes contain all the receptive models for listening and reading, the conversations, the vocabulary presentations, the Listening with a Purpose texts, the reading texts, and the pronunciation presentations and practices from the student's book. The audiocassettes provide space for student practice and self-correction.

**Videocassette**   The videocassette, *True Voices,* contains a unique combination of controlled and improvised dramatic episodes that support the social language and grammar in the *True Colors* student's book. In addition, students see a video magazine of scenes depicting the themes touched on throughout the student's book (shopping, working, etc.) and on-the-street interviews about the same topics and themes.

**Video Workbook**   A video workbook provides active language practice and reinforcement of all social language and grammar from the video.

**Achievement Tests**   Achievement tests offer opportunities for evaluation of student progress on a unit-by-unit basis. In addition, a placement test is available to aid in placing groups in one of the five levels of *True Colors*: Basic, Book 1, Book 2, Book 3, or Book 4.

## Student's Book Unit Contents

**Photo Story**   An illustrated conversation or story provokes interest, provides enjoyment, and demonstrates the use of target language in authentic, natural speech. This rich model of real speech can be presented as a reading or a listening. It is purposely designed to be a slight step ahead of students' productive ability because students can understand more than they can produce, and the EFL student needs abundant authentic models of native speech.

*Comprehension*   Questions about the conversation focus on the key comprehension skills of factual recall, confirmation of content, identifying main ideas, drawing conclusions, and understanding meaning from context. These can serve as listening comprehension or reading comprehension exercises.

**Social Language and Grammar Lessons**
Short, numbered lessons form the instructional core of each unit of *True Colors*. Social language and grammar are tightly linked in each of these mini-lessons, through the following combination of presentations and opportunities for practice:

*Conversation*   A short dialogue at the students' productive level presents and models important social language.

*Pair Practice*   The same dialogue is presented for student practice with opportunities for personalization of the social language. This limited opportunity for manipulation is the first step toward ownership of the language that is the goal and promise of *True Colors* .

*Vocabulary*   Illustrated and captioned vocabulary presentations within each unit provide students with important words to make their own. Students are not asked to guess the meaning of the unit's active vocabulary; instead, *True Colors* presents a clear illustration to convey meaning and follows it with opportunities for practice and free production.

*Grammar*   Clear, well-explained grammar presentations are integrated with the social language and support comprehension and production of it. These grammar presentations never occur in isolation but rather form a support for the social language of the lesson, giving the grammar both meaning and purpose. To this end, grammar exercises are set in a context that supports the communicative focus of the lesson.

 A major goal of *True Colors* is to teach students to improvise based on the language they already know. Improvisation is the "fifth skill"—the one students need to master in order to move out of the pages of a textbook and into the real world. Through a continuum of freer and freer opportunities for language ownership, *True Colors* students put the course into their own words, **letting their own true colors shine through.**

**Pronunciation**   Each unit isolates a basic and important feature of the pronunciation or intonation of spoken American English. Practice is structured into games and into listening, speaking, and dictation activities.

**Game or Info-Gap**   Each unit contains at least one interactive language activity that activates grammar, social language, vocabulary, or pronunciation.

**Listening with a Purpose**   In addition to the recorded texts in the unit, one or two additional listening texts provide another receptive model a step above students' productive ability. A two-step comprehension syllabus centers on two essential listening skills—determining context and focusing attention. Through a unique and rigorous approach to listening comprehension similar to the reading comprehension skills of skimming and scanning, students build their ability to understand at a level above what is normally expected of false beginners.

**Reading**   Each unit provides practice in the reading skill with texts slightly above students' productive ability. Topics are especially devised to create motivated readers, and each reading is followed by further comprehension practice in all the comprehension sub skills.

   This unique and exciting culminating activity systematically builds students' ability to express their own opinions, ideas, and feelings on a variety of topics. Carefully designed questions provoke interest without soliciting production above students' level. Each Heart to Heart activity comes near the end of the unit, ensuring adequate preparation for success.

**Writing**   Writing activities in each unit provide real and realistic writing tasks that reinforce the target language in the writing skill while providing additional opportunities for personal expression.

   This full-page illustration ends each unit and has been especially drawn to elicit from students all the language they have learned within the unit—the vocabulary, the social language, the grammar, and the thematic contexts. Students begin talking about the contents of this picture early in the unit and continue throughout the unit. At the end of the unit, they ask each other questions about the actions depicted, they make true and false statements about what they see, they create conversations for the characters, they tell stories about what is happening—all IN THEIR OWN WORDS. All students, regardless of ability, will succeed at their own levels because what the students know how to say has been drawn into the illustration and what they don't know how to say has been purposely left out.

**Review units**   These units are provided after unit five (mid-book) and at the end. They provide review, self-tests, extra classroom practice, and a social language self-test.

**Appendices**   The key vocabulary, spelling rules, and noun and verb charts are organized and presented at the end of the book for easy reference and test preparation.

# About the Authors and Series Director

## Authors

### Jay Maurer

Jay Maurer has taught English in Binational Centers, colleges, and universities in Portugal, Spain, Mexico, the Somali Republic, and the United States. In addition, he taught intensive English at Columbia University's American Language Program.

Dr. Maurer has an M.A. and an M. Ed. in Applied Linguistics as well as a Ph. D. in The Teaching of English, all from Columbia University. In addition to this new adult and young adult English course, he is the author of the Advanced Level of Longman's widely acclaimed *Focus on Grammar* series and co-author of the three-level *Structure Practice in Context* series. Dr. Maurer teaches and writes in the Seattle, Washington, area and recently conducted a series of teaching workshops in Brazil and Japan.

### Irene E. Schoenberg

Irene E. Schoenberg has taught English to international students for over twenty years at Hunter College's International Language Institute and at Columbia University's American Language Program. Additionally, she trains English instructors in EFL/ESL teaching methods at The New School for Social Research. Her M.A. is in TESOL from Columbia University. She is a popular speaker to national and international TESOL groups.

Professor Schoenberg is the author of the Basic Level of the *Focus on Grammar* series as well as the author of the two engaging, unique, and widely-used conversation texts, *Talk About Trivia* and *Talk About Values*. In addition to *True Colors,* Professor Schoenberg is developing a new visual dictionary for learners of English.

## Series Director

### Joan Saslow

Joan Saslow has taught English and foreign languages to adults and young adults in both South America and the United States. She taught English at the Binational Centers of Valparaíso and Viña del Mar, Chile, and English and French at the Catholic University of Valparaíso. She taught English as a Foreign Language to Japanese university students at Marymount College and to international students in Westchester Community College's intensive program.

Ms. Saslow is the author of *English in Context: Reading Comprehension for Science and Technology,* a three-level text series. In addition, Ms. Saslow has been an editor of language teaching materials, a teacher trainer, and a frequent speaker at gatherings of English teachers outside the United States for twenty-five years.

# Are you in this class?

**W**arm up: Look at the pictures. Where are these people—in a class or at home?
Read or listen. 🎧

But the class is hard. Right, Mary?

Not for me. I'm the teacher.

## Vocabulary • Nouns for Talking About People

🎧 *Look at the pictures. Say each word.*

**a teacher**

**a student**

**friends**

**neighbors**

## Comprehension: Confirming Content

*Mark the following statements **true**, **false**, or **I don't know**.*

|  |  | True | False | I don't know. |
|---|---|:---:|:---:|:---:|
| **Example:** | Amy and Bob are friends. | ☑ | ☐ | ☐ |
| **1.** | Amy and Bob are students. | ☐ | ☐ | ☐ |
| **2.** | This is an English class. | ☐ | ☐ | ☐ |
| **3.** | Bob is married. | ☐ | ☐ | ☐ |
| **4.** | Mary is a student. | ☐ | ☐ | ☐ |
| **5.** | Mary is an easy teacher. | ☐ | ☐ | ☐ |

# **H**OW TO **make informal introductions and talk about occupations**

## Verb Be: Use and Form

**statements**

I'**m** a teacher.

This *is* my friend Bob.

He'**s** a student.

We'**re** in this class.

Bill, Bob, and Jean **are** my friends.

They'**re** all students.

| subject pronoun | verb | | contraction (short form) |
|---|---|---|---|
| | | singular | |
| I | *am* | ⟶ | I'*m* |
| you | *are* | ⟶ | you'*re* |
| he | *is* | ⟶ | he'*s* |
| she | *is* | ⟶ | she'*s* |
| it | *is* | ⟶ | it'*s* |
| | | plural | |
| we | *are* | ⟶ | we'*re* |
| you | *are* | ⟶ | you'*re* |
| they | *are* | ⟶ | they'*re* |

**GRAMMAR TASK:** Find and circle all the subject pronouns in the photo story on pages 2-3.

## Conversation 1

🎧 *Read and listen to the conversation.*

**A:** Hi. My name's Bill Blake.

**B:** Hi, Bill. Nice to meet you.

**A:** Nice to meet you, too.

🎧 *Listen again and practice.*

## Pair Practice

*Practice introductions with a partner. Learn your classmates' names.*

**A:** Hi. My name's _____.

**B:** Hi, _____. Nice to meet you.

**A:** Nice to meet you, too.

## Conversation 2

🎧 *Read and listen to the conversation.*

**A:** Sally, this is my friend Steve. Steve, this is Sally.
**B:** Hi, Sally. Nice to meet you.
**C:** Nice to meet you, too.

🎧 *Listen again and practice.*

## Pair Practice

*Practice introductions with two partners. Use their names.*

**A:** _____, this is my friend _____. _____, this is _____.

**B:** Hi, _____. Nice to meet you.

**C:** Nice to meet you, too.

☑ **Now you know how to make informal introductions.**

## Vocabulary • Occupations

🎧 *Look at the pictures. Say each word.*

**a doctor**  **a homemaker**  **a lawyer**  **a nurse**  **a secretary**

**a student**  **a manager**  **an engineer**  **an artist**

## Conversation 3

🎧 *Read and listen to the conversation.*

**A:** Nice party.
**B:** Yeah, it's great.
**A:** So what do you do, Nadia?
**B:** I'm a nurse. What about you?
**A:** I'm an engineer.

🎧 *Listen again and practice.*

## Pair Practice

*Practice the conversation and vocabulary with a partner.*
*Use your own words.*

**A:** Nice party.

**B:** Yeah, it's great.

**A:** So what do you do, _____?

**B:** I'm _____. What about you?

**A:** I'm _____.

☑ **Now you know how to talk about occupations.**

 Look at the picture on page 13. Talk about the picture with a partner. Create a conversation. Use your own words.

SOCIAL LANGUAGE AND GRAMMAR 2

# HOW TO ask questions/make negative statements about people and things

### Questions with Be

| *yes-no questions* | possible answers |
|---|---|
| Are you in this class? | Yes, I am. |
| Are you a student? | No, I'm not. I'm the teacher. |
| Is Mary a teacher? | Yes, she is. |
| Is the class hard? | No, it's not. (*or* No, it isn't.) |
| Am I late? | No, you're not. |

**TIP:** Don't contract affirmative short answers: ***Yes, it is.*** (~~*not* Yes, it's.~~)

| *wh- questions* | possible answers |
|---|---|
| What's your name? | Katherine Baker. |
| Who's the teacher? | Mary Stanton. |

**GRAMMAR TASK:** Answer the same two questions in your own words.

### Negative Statements with Be

She'**s *not*** the teacher. (*or* She ***isn't*** the teacher.)

I'***m not*** Bob.

We'***re not*** at home now. (*or* We ***aren't*** at home now.)

## Grammar in a Context

Complete the conversation with the following words.

| how's | I'm | is | Is | she's not | It's | What's |
|-------|-----|-----|-----|-----------|------|--------|
| it is | It's | she's | am | Are | We're | is |

Amy? Come on! _____ all at
**1.**
the dinner table. Dinner's ready.

OK, Mom. Sorry
_____ late.
**2.**

So _____
**3.**
your class this
semester, Amy?

Fine, Dad. _____ great. And the new teacher
**4.**
_____ really nice and very interesting—not boring.
**5.**

_____ her name?
**6.**

Ms. Stanton.
But we all call
her Mary.

Mary? But
Mary _____
**7.**
a first name!

Yes, that's right, _____. But _____
**8.** **9.**
pretty young. _____ OK.
**10.**

_____ you sure?
**11.**

Yeah, Mom.
I _____.
**12.**

And what about Sally? _____ she
in the class, too? **13.**

No, _____.
**14.**

 **Look at the picture on page 13. Make true and false statements
about the picture. Your partner corrects the false statements.**

# Reading

## A Newspaper Article

*Before You Read: Ask your teacher,*
*"Where are you from?"*

*Read the newspaper article.* 🎧

## Comprehension: Factual Recall

*Match the following words and phrases.*

1. Mary Stanton     a state
2. Phillip Stanton     a city
3. Colorado     an instructor
4. Sacramento     an engineer
5. twenty-four     Mary's age
6. engineer     skiers
7. Mary and Phillip     Phillip's occupation

## • Centerville Gazette •

### Who's New?

We welcome Mary Stanton. Ms. Stanton is a new instructor here this year. "Centerville students are really interesting people," she says. "They're young and old, married and single. My classes are all interesting."

Mary and her husband, Phillip, are new to Colorado. They're from Sacramento, California. Phillip is an engineer for Dynamo Labs. Ms. Stanton says, "Colorado is wonderful! It's a great state, especially for skiers like Phil and me."

Mary is young. She's only twenty-four years old.

She says, "Sometimes students think I'm a student. They call me Mary. That's OK—if they're respectful. And sometimes they think I'm an easy teacher because I'm young. But they're wrong!"

Welcome to Centerville, Ms. Mary Stanton!

---

SOCIAL LANGUAGE AND GRAMMAR 3

# How to describe people

### Indefinite and Definite Articles: A, An, The

Nouns are the names of persons, places, or things.

Use **a** or **an** with singular nouns.

singular noun      plural noun
Amy is **a student**. Amy and Bob are **students**.

Use **a** before a consonant sound.

    **a t**eenager

Use **an** before a vowel sound.

    **an** adult

Compare **a** and **the** in these examples.

    Mary's **a** teacher.

    Mary's **the** teacher.

Use **the** (not **a** or **an**) for specific persons or things.

**a teenager / an adult**

**a student / a teacher**

**GRAMMAR TASK:** Find and circle examples of **a** and **an** in the newspaper article about Mary. Then circle each noun that follows.

## **Vocabulary** • Nouns and Adjectives That Describe People

🎧 *Look at the pictures. Say each word.*

**a man / a woman**

**a teenager / an adult**

**a student / a teacher**

**athletic / studious**

**young / old**

**married / single**

**tall / short**

**In Your Own Words**

**Talk about the picture on page 13 with a partner. Examples: "He's short." "She's a teenager." Use your own words.**

**Heart to Heart**

*I think...*    *In my opinion...*    *because...*

*Circle the vocabulary words that describe you.*

| | | | |
|---|---|---|---|
| **a man** | **a woman** | **a teenager** | **an adult** |
| **a student** | **a teacher** | **athletic** | **studious** |
| **married** | **single** | **young** | **old** |
| **tall** | **short** | | |

*Now, with a partner, ask and answer personal questions.*

**Examples:**  Are you athletic? Are you studious?

Are you married or single?

Are your classes hard?

Is your occupation interesting or boring?

*I feel...*    *I don't think...*    *What about you?*

# Listening with a Purpose

## Focus Attention

*Read these words.*

| | | | | |
|---|---|---|---|---|
| an animal | a human | married | single | Brazilian |
| American | real | fictional | old | young |
| athletic | studious | historical | a superhero | |

🎧 *Look at the picture. Listen to the TV quiz program. Listen for the words.*

PANELISTS

CONTESTANT #1

🎧 *Now listen again. Look at the words again and circle each word or phrase when you hear it.*

**TIP:** Circle only the words you hear. The other words are not on the tape.

## Who Am I?

*(reinforces describing people)*

*Work in pairs. One student selects a fictional or historical character. The other student guesses who it is.*

> **Example:** **A:** Are you a man?
>
> **B:** Yes, I am, *etc.*

*Then, with your partner, describe the character to the other pairs. They guess who it is.*

> **Example:** The character is a man / a woman.
> He's / She's . . .

# Pronunciation

## The Alphabet

🎧 *Listen to the pronunciation of the letters.*

**Capital letters**

A B C D E F G H I J K L M N O P Q R S T U V W X Y Z

**Lower-case letters**

a b c d e f g h i j k l m n o p q r s t u v w x y z

🎧 *Listen again and repeat.*

🎧 *Now listen and write the names the speaker spells. Begin each name with a capital letter.*

**1.** _____    **3.** _____

**2.** _____    **4.** _____

*Now spell your last name for a partner. Your partner writes your name here:*

_____

# Infocode

*(reinforces meaning of first and last names)*

*Write your last name in code.*

**Example:** Fox = 6 – 15 – 24    (F=6    O = 15    X = 24)

| A | B | C | D | E | F | G | H | I | J | K | L | M |
|---|---|---|---|---|---|---|---|---|---|---|---|---|
| 1 | 2 | 3 | 4 | 5 | 6 | 7 | 8 | 9 | 10 | 11 | 12 | 13 |

| N | O | P | Q | R | S | T | U | V | W | X | Y | Z |
|---|---|---|---|---|---|---|---|---|---|---|---|---|
| 14 | 15 | 16 | 17 | 18 | 19 | 20 | 21 | 22 | 23 | 24 | 25 | 26 |

_____

Your last name in code

**Improvise**

*You know your classmates' first names. Circulate around the room.*
*Decode your classmates' last names. Then spell the names out loud.*

# ◤ **Writing**
### Addressing an Envelope

*Bruce is Bob's big brother. He is an English teacher in Chile.*
*Look at the envelope from Bruce's letter to Bob.*

Bruce Mercer
Ecuador 261
Viña del Mar, Chile

Bob Mercer
611 Elm Street
Centerville, CO 80901
U.S.A.

**Correo Aéreo**
**Airmail**

*Complete the sentences in Bob's answer to his brother Bruce.*
*Use contractions when possible.*

September 5

Dear Bruce,

   Hi! Thanks for your letter. How'_____ Chile? _____ you

very busy? How'_____ the skiing? Wow, skiing in September. Cool.

   I have five classes this semester. _____ all good, and my

teachers _____ all terrific, especially Mary Stanton. You don't

know her. _____ new. _____ great, and she'_____ very

young. Her classes _____ really interesting.

   Well, _____ late for dinner. Write soon.

         Bob

*Now address the envelope to*
*Bruce. Use Bob's address as the*
*return address. Look at Bruce's*
*envelope as a model. Use capital*
*letters for names of people and*
*places. Use a comma (,) after*
*the city.*

**W**arm up: Talk about this picture with a partner.
• Talk about the people. • What are their occupations?
• Ask your partner questions with **who.** • Describe the
people: young, old, teenager, etc. • What are they saying?

**T**hen: Create conversations for the people. OR Tell a story
about the picture. Say as much as you can.

13

# There's a noise downstairs!

Receptive Model

**Warm up:** Look at the pictures. Is it daytime or nighttime? Read or listen. 🎧

Hello?

Diana, this is Sandy.

Oh . . . Sandy. It's two o'clock in the morning! What's wrong?

Diana, I'm scared.

Scared? Why are you scared <u>this</u> time?

There's a noise downstairs. I'm sure there's someone in the house. I'm really scared.

## Comprehension: Factual Recall

*Circle the correct letter.*

**1.** Who are Diana and Sandy?

   **a.** They're friends.      **b.** They're burglars.

**2.** Is there a burglar in Sandy's house?

   **a.** Yes, there is.      **b.** No, there isn't.

**3.** What is the problem in Sandy's house?

   **a.** There's a burglar.      **b.** There's a noise.

# **H**OW **TO say the time**

## **Vocabulary** • **Telling Time**

🎧 *Look at the pictures. Say each time.*

2:00 = It's two o'clock.

2:07 = It's two-oh-seven.

2:15 = It's two-fifteen *or* a quarter after two.

2:25 = It's two-twenty-five *or* twenty-five after two.

2:30 = It's two-thirty *or* half past two.

2:45 = It's two-forty-five *or* a quarter to three.

2:55 = It's two-fifty-five *or* five to three.

*Receptive Model*

# **L**istening with a Purpose

## **Focus Attention**

*Look at this chart of theaters, movies, and times.*

| THEATER | MOVIE | SHOWTIME IN NUMBERS | SHOWTIME IN WORDS* |
|---------|-------|---------------------|---------------------|
| Theater 1 | *My Favorite Vampire* | | |
| Theater 1 | *Invaders from the Underground* | | |
| Theater 2 | *Son of Dracula* | | |
| Theater 2 | *Elephant Woman* | | |

🎧 *Listen to the movie announcement.*

🎧 *Now listen again. Fill in the "showtime in numbers" column. Then write the showtime in words.*

\* **B**onus **Question**: Can you write each time in another way?

# **H**OW TO **identify yourself on the phone/ask how someone is**

## **Conversation**

 *Read and listen to the conversation.*

**A:** Hello?

**B:** Carol, hi. This is Jennifer.

**A:** Oh hi, Jennifer. How are you?

**B:** Fine. I'm so excited.

**A:** Excited? Why?

**B:** *Elephant Woman* is at the Cineplex.

**A:** It is? That's great.

 *Listen again and practice.*

## **Pair Practice**

*Practice the conversation with a partner.
Use your own words.*

**A:** Hello?

**B:** _____, hi. This is _____.

**A:** Oh hi, _____. How are you?

**B:** Fine. I'm so excited.

**A:** Excited? Why?

**B:** _____ is at the Cineplex.

**A:** It is? That's great.

☑ **Now you know how to identify yourself on the telephone and ask how someone is.**

 **Look at the picture on page 25. Make true and false statements about the movies in the picture. Your partner corrects the false statements. Use your own words.**

# How to make plans to meet

## Conversation

🎧 *Read and listen to the conversation.*

**A:** There's a good movie at the Lido tonight.
**B:** What is it?
**A:** *Son of Dracula.* Do you want to go?
**B:** Maybe. What time?
**A:** Seven o'clock.
**B:** OK. See you there.
**A:** Terrific. See you later.
**B:** Bye.

🎧 *Listen again and practice.*

## Pair Practice

*Practice the conversation with a partner. Use this chart for ideas. Use your own words.*

| what? (events) | | | when? | what time? |
|---|---|---|---|---|
| a movie | a play | a concert | today | 8:00 |
| | | | tonight | 7:45 |
| | | | tomorrow | 6:20 |

**TIP:** Use *at* for locations and for times: *There's a concert **at the theater at 8:00.***

**A:** There's a good _____ at the Lido _____.

**B:** What is it?

**A:** _____. Do you want to go?

**B:** Maybe. What time?

**A:** _____.

**B:** OK. See you there.

**A:** Terrific. See you later.

**B:** Bye.

☑ **Now you know how to make plans to meet.**

**Vocabulary** • Prepositions for Times of the Day and Dates

🎧 *Look at the pictures. Say each phrase.*

***in the* morning**

***in the* afternoon**

***in the* evening**

***on* July fourth**

Look at the schedule of events. Tell your partner about an
event. Invite him or her to do something. Use this schedule
of events and your own words and ideas.

**Events This Week**

| Monday | Tuesday | Wednesday | Thursday | Friday | Saturday | Sunday |
|---|---|---|---|---|---|---|
| Guitar Concert Theater, 7:30 P.M. | Basketball Game Gym, 11 A.M. | Movie "War of the Worlds" Theater, 6:45 P.M. | Soccer Game Stadium, 3:30 P.M. | Rock Concert Theater, 8 P.M. | Play "Hamlet" Theater, 7 P.M. | Class Picnic Central Park, Noon |

**Look at the pictures on page 25. Talk about the pictures with a
partner. What is the man saying? Use your own words.**

# **H**OW TO **describe things and places**

---

**Count and Non-count Nouns: There Is / There Are**

Nouns are the names of persons, places, or things.

A *count noun* is a noun you can count.

> one *book*, two *students*, ten *women*

Use *a* or *an* with a singular count noun.

> *a cat*

Use *there's (there is)* with a singular count noun.

> *There's a cat* in the house.

Use *there are* with a plural count noun.

> *There are two bedrooms* in this house.

A *non-count noun* is a noun that names a thing you cannot count.

> *music, air, information, bread, water*

Use *there's (there is)* with non-count nouns.

> *There's water* on the floor.

---

▼ **TIP:** Do not use *a* or *an* before a non-count noun.

---

▼ **GRAMMAR TASK:** Find and circle a sentence with *there is* or *there are* in "A Mystery Planet" on page 23.

---

## **Practice**

*Look at the pictures. Write the four count nouns together.*
*Write the four non-count nouns together.*

 water     bread     elephant     car

 milk     orange     snow     dog

**COUNT NOUNS**              **NON-COUNT NOUNS**

_____    |    _____

_____    |    _____

## Grammar in a Context

*Welcome to Strange World. Find thirteen strange things in Strange World. Write **there is** or **there are** in the blanks. Use **a** or **an** if necessary.*

Strange World

Everything is strange in Strange World. _____ two moons in the sky, and _____
　　　　　　　　　　　　　　　　　　　　　　　　　　　　1.　　　　　　　　　　　　　　　　　　　　2.

ring around one of the moons. In this house, _____ car in the kitchen. _____
　　　　　　　　　　　　　　　　　　　　　　　　　3.　　　　　　　　　　　　　　4.

three telephones on the ceiling. _____ cat at the dining room table. _____ ice
　　　　　　　　　　　　　　　　　　　5.　　　　　　　　　　　　　　　　　　6.

in the kitchen, and _____ snow in the dining room. _____ bread in the glass,
　　　　　　　　　　　　7.　　　　　　　　　　　　　　　　　　8.

and _____ water on the plate. _____ tree in the living room. _____
　　　　　9.　　　　　　　　　　　　10.　　　　　　　　　　　　　　　　　11.

apples, oranges, and bananas on the tree. _____ elephant in the tree. _____
　　　　　　　　　　　　　　　　　　　　　　12.　　　　　　　　　　　　　　13.

dog in the tree, too. Strange World is a very strange place.

**Look at the room in the picture on page 25. With a partner, ask and answer questions about the room. Use *Is there* and *Are there*.**

# Listening with a Purpose

## Determine Context

🎧 *Listen to the conversation. Make notes on this chart.*

| Who? | Where? | What? |
|------|--------|-------|
|      |        |       |

🎧 *Now listen to the conversation again. Circle the correct letter.*

**1.** Who wants to buy something?

    **a.** the man         **b.** the woman

**2.** Where is the conversation taking place?

    **a.** in an airport     **b.** on the telephone

**3.** What is the subject of the conversation?

    **a.** seats for a flight     **b.** seats for a concert

## Focus Attention

🎧 *Now listen again. Check the statement or question in each pair that you hear in the conversation.*

**1.** ☐ There are three flights today, sir.

    ☐ There are three flights every day, sir.

**2.** ☐ Yes, there are seats available, but only in the nonsmoking section.

    ☐ Yes, there are seats available, but only in the smoking section.

**3.** ☐ Well, is there a window seat available?

    ☐ Well, there is a window seat available.

**4.** ☐ What about my seat?

    ☐ What about an aisle seat?

**5.** ☐ That's great. I'll take it.

    ☐ That's great. We'll take it.

## Crazy Backwards Questions
*(reinforces questions with **be**)*

*Partner B, turn to page 144.*
*Partner A, here is a list of five answers. Read each one to Partner B.*
*Partner B gives you a question for each answer.*

**Example:** **A:** Three-thirty.
**B:** What time is it?

1. **A:** Mary Stanton.
2. **A:** Eight-ten.
3. **A:** Yes, I am.
4. **A:** They're really boring.
5. **A:** At the Lido.

*Partner A, now here is a list of five questions for Partner B's answers.*

6. **A:** Is there a cat in this house?
7. **A:** How are you?
8. **A:** Is he married?
9. **A:** Who's that?
10. **A:** What's playing at the Cineplex?

# Reading

## Short Paragraphs

**B**efore You Read: *Think about the names of all the planets you know.*
*Read the paragraph and guess the mystery planet.*

## A Mystery Planet

Planet X is a very cold planet. There's ice here and maybe snow. It's also a very large planet. It's far from the sun—more than 1.4 billion kilometers. There are a lot of moons around Planet X—more than twenty. And there are rings around Planet X.

Is there life on Planet X? No one knows.

What planet is it? _____
ANSWER: SATURN

## Comprehension: Identifying the Main Idea

*Choose another title for **A Mystery Planet.***

**a.** The Planet with Life          **b.** The Planet with Rings

**Heart to Heart**

In my opinion... I think... because...

Tell a partner about your favorite place. Make a list of reasons. Use **there is** and **there are.** Compare your list with a partner's list. Then make a class chart of favorite places and reasons.

I feel... I don't think... What about you?

## **W**riting

### A Short Note to a Classmate

*You want to go to the movies with a classmate tonight.*

*Look at the movie schedule on page 16. Invite your classmate with a short note.*

*Remember to use a capital letter for names of people, places, and titles. Remember to use a period at the end of sentences. Use a question mark (?) at the end of questions.*

FROM THE DESK OF
KEN TANAKA

Hi, Monica:

"My Favorite Vampire" is playing at the Lido today. There's a show at 4:45. Do you want to go?

Ken

## **P**ronunciation

/s/ , /z/ , /ɪz/

🎧 *Listen to these plural nouns. Listen especially for the last sound in the word.*

| /s/ | /z/ | /ɪz/ |
|-----|-----|------|
| elephants | animals | nurses |
| students | dogs | classes |
| cats | days | noises |
| flights | neighbors | places |

🎧 *Listen again and repeat.*

🎧 *Now listen to the words and write them in the correct columns.*

| ends in /s/ | ends in /z/ | ends in /ɪz/ |
|-------------|-------------|--------------|
| _____ | _____ | _____ |
| _____ | _____ | _____ |
| _____ | _____ | _____ |
| _____ | _____ | _____ |

**W**arm up: Talk about these pictures with a partner.
• Talk about the people. • What are they saying?
• Where are they? • What things are in the picture?
• Ask questions with **Is there** and **Are there**.

**T**hen: Create conversations for the people. OR Tell a
story about the picture. Say as much as you can.

**Receptive Model**

Hi, honey. I'm home.

Oh, Frank. What a day! The fax machine is broken.

Oh no. Not again! Well, let's call the help number. And then let's go out to eat.

OK. What's the number?

It's on the machine.

"Terrific Technology." Thank you for calling our Help Line. Please press ONE now. Thank you.

For computer questions, press ONE now.

For new products, press TWO now.

BEEP!

For a list of stores in your area, press THREE now.

To leave a message, press FOUR now.

To speak to a representative, press FIVE now.

Our representatives are all busy. Please don't hang up.

BEEP!

## Comprehension: Confirming Content

*Mark the following statements* **true**, **false**, *or* **I don't know**.

|  |  | True | False | I don't know. |
|---|---|:---:|:---:|:---:|
| **Example:** | Joanne and Frank have a fax machine. | ☑ | ☐ | ☐ |
| **1.** | Their fax machine is broken. | ☐ | ☐ | ☐ |
| **2.** | Joanne and Frank are at home. | ☐ | ☐ | ☐ |
| **3.** | The representatives are all busy. | ☐ | ☐ | ☐ |
| **4.** | Joanne is angry. | ☐ | ☐ | ☐ |

# **H**OW TO **suggest an activity/an alternative**

| Commands and Suggestions with *Let's* | | |
|---|---|---|
| **affirmative commands** | **negative commands** | **contraction** |
| *Press* five. | *Don't hang up.* | *don't* = do not |
| *Be* here at 6:00. | *Don't be* late. | |
| **suggestions with *let's*** | | |
| *Let's go* to a movie. | *Let's not* watch a video. | |

**TIP**: Use *please* with commands to be polite.

   *Please* press five.

   *Please* don't be late.

**GRAMMAR TASK:** Find and circle commands in the photo story on pages 26–27.

## **Conversation**

🎧 *Read and listen to the conversation.*

**A:** Let's go to a movie tonight.

**B:** No, let's not go out. Let's watch a video instead.

**A:** Oh, all right. But I'm really hungry. Do you want to order a pizza?

**B:** OK. How about Mario's?

**A:** Good idea. Call Mario's.

🎧 *Listen again and practice.*

## **Vocabulary** • Social Activities

🎧 *Look at the pictures. Say each phrase.*

go to a (rock) concert

go to a restaurant

go for a walk

go to a play

## Pair Practice

*Practice the conversation and vocabulary with a partner. Use your own words.*

**A:** Let's _____ tonight.

**B:** No, let's not go out. Let's _____ instead.

**A:** Oh, all right. But I'm really hungry. Do you want to order a pizza?

**B:** OK. How about _____?

**A:** Good idea. Call _____.

☑ **Now you know how to suggest an activity and an alternative.**

 **Look at the picture on page 37. Create a conversation for the man and the woman. Use your own words.**

## Pronunciation

### Stress and Meaning

Look at how stress affects meaning:

> Let's *call* them. (Let's not write them a letter.)
>
> Let's call *them*. (Let's not call someone else.)

🎧 *Listen to the following pairs of sentences. Circle the word with the most stress.*

  **a.** Let's call them.

  **b.** Let's call them.

🎧 *Now listen again. Circle the letter of the correct explanation.*

**1.** Let's walk to the movies.

  **a.** Let's walk to the movies, not any other place.

  **b.** Let's walk to the movies, not drive.

**2.** Let's walk to the movies.

  **a.** Let's walk to the movies, not any other place.

  **b.** Let's walk to the movies, not drive.

*Make a list of five activities you like.*

**Examples:** playing sports, walking, going to the movies, etc.

*Make suggestions to a partner to go somewhere. If you don't like an activity, say why not and suggest an alternative.*

**Example:** **A:** Let's walk on the beach.

**B:** No, let's not. It's cold today.

Let's _____ instead.

SOCIAL LANGUAGE AND GRAMMAR 2

# HOW TO state your address and telephone number

## Possessive Adjectives and Possessive Nouns

*My* address is 75 Jones Street.

The *teacher's* phone number is 232-1748.

### possessive adjectives

my
your
his
her
its
our
their

**TIP:** Make subjects and possessive adjectives agree.

*He* is in *his* room, and *she* is in *her* room.

### possessive nouns

Use *'s* to make singular nouns possessive.

My sister*'s* office is closed.

Louis*'s* fax machine is broken.

Use an apostrophe (') to make a plural noun ending in *s* possessive.

Her parent*s'* telephone number is 724-3636.

Use *'s* for plural nouns that don't end in *s*.

The children*'s* cat is outside.

**GRAMMAR TASK:** Find and circle possessive adjectives in the photo story on pages 26–27.

## Grammar in a Context

*Complete the conversations with the correct possessive adjectives or possessive nouns.*

**1. Mom:** Sally, where are you? _____ friends are here.
<u>Their / Your</u>

**Sally:** I'm up in _____ room, Mom.
<u>my / its</u>

**2. Dad:** Let's go, kids. _____ flight is at 10:00.
<u>Our / Its</u>

**Jessica:** Jimmy's not ready, Dad. He's still in _____ room.
<u>his / her</u>

**3. Doctor's Office:** Dr. _____ office. May I help you?
<u>Stones / Stone's</u>

**Mr. Stanley:** Yes, my daughter is sick. _____ temperature is 40 degrees.
<u>Her / Your</u>

**Doctor's Office:** You need to speak to Dr. Stone.

**4. Dad:** Is this a children's book?

**Mom:** I think so. _____ title is *Goodnight Moon.*
<u>Its / My</u>

**5. Miranda:** Is there a party at your _____ house?
<u>grandparents' / grandparents</u>

**Paul:** Yes, it's _____ 50th wedding anniversary.
<u>your / their</u>

## Conversation

🎧 *Read and listen to the conversation.*

**A:** This fax machine is broken.
**B:** No problem. Your name, please?
**A:** Joanne Tanaka.
**B:** Could you spell that, please?
**A:** Sure. T-A-N-A-K-A.
**B:** And your address?
**A:** 1640 Barkley Street.
**B:** Phone number?
**A:** 694-7021.
**B:** OK, Ms. Tanaka. I'll give you a call when it's ready.

🎧 *Listen again and practice.*

## Vocabulary • Machines and Appliances

🎧 *Look at the pictures. Say each word or phrase.*

**a fax machine**       **a computer**       **a laptop**       **a remote**

**a TV**       **a CD player**       **a cassette player**       **a VCR**

## Pair Practice

*Practice the conversation and vocabulary with a partner. Use your own words.*

**A:** This _____ is broken.

**B:** No problem. Your name, please?

**A:** _____.

**B:** Could you spell that, please?

**A:** Sure. _____.

**B:** And your address?

**A:** _____.

**B:** Phone number?

**A:** _____.

**B:** OK, _____. I'll give you a call when it's ready.

☑ **Now you know how to give your address and telephone number.**

**Look at the picture on page 37. Tell a partner the names of the machines in the living room.**

# HOW TO describe family relationships

## Vocabulary • Family Relationships

🎧 *Look at the pictures. Say each word.*

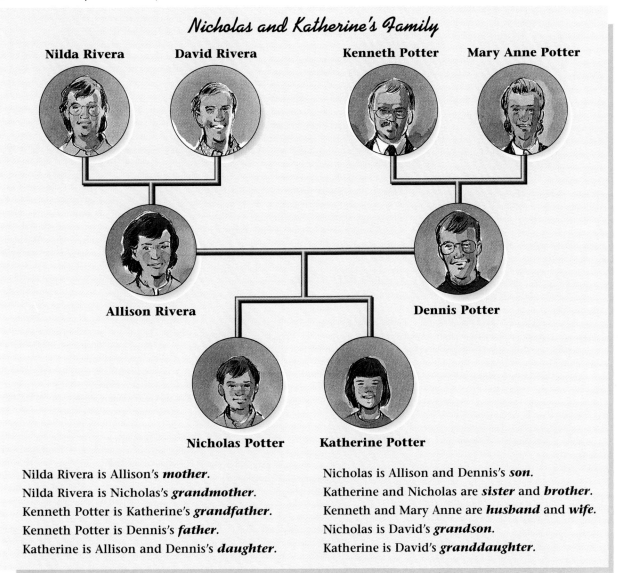

*Nicholas and Katherine's Family*

**Nilda Rivera**    **David Rivera**    **Kenneth Potter**    **Mary Anne Potter**

**Allison Rivera**    **Dennis Potter**

**Nicholas Potter**    **Katherine Potter**

Nilda Rivera is Allison's *mother*.

Nilda Rivera is Nicholas's *grandmother*.

Kenneth Potter is Katherine's *grandfather*.

Kenneth Potter is Dennis's *father*.

Katherine is Allison and Dennis's *daughter*.

Nicholas is Allison and Dennis's *son*.

Katherine and Nicholas are *sister* and *brother*.

Kenneth and Mary Anne are *husband* and *wife*.

Nicholas is David's *grandson*.

Katherine is David's *granddaughter*.

## Grammar and Vocabulary with a Partner

*Work with a partner. Write more sentences about this family and their relationships.*
*Then compare your sentences with other classmates' sentences.*

**Example:**    David is Nilda's husband.

 **Look at the picture on page 37. Find a photograph of this family. Talk about the people in the photograph.**

# Reading

### Advertisements

*B*efore You Read: *Are there advertisements like these in your town or city?*

*Read the advertisements on the bulletin board.* 🎧

### Comprehension: Factual Recall

*Complete each statement by circling the correct letter.*

1. The car stereo cassette player is _____.
   **a.** new          **b.** Kim's

2. The laptop is _____.
   **a.** new          **b.** not new

3. 232-1776 is Jerome's _____.
   **a.** telephone number   **b.** address

4. The _____ of the language lab is 60 State Street.
   **a.** phone number      **b.** address

5. The cassette player is _____.
   **a.** Jerome's          **b.** Fred's

For Sale
Cheap
CD player
Like new
332-9979

Fax Machine
**Great Condition**
**$50**

**Call 543-8828 after five o'clock.**

CASSETTE PLAYER
NEW
SPEAK TO FRED AT THE LANGUAGE LAB.
60 STATE STREET

For Sale
Car stereo cassette player
1 year old
666-4242
Ask for Kim.

**Don't rent. Buy!**
My laptop is in terrific condition.
Call Jerome at 232-1776 evenings.

## Vocabulary • Classroom Commands

🎧 *Look at the pictures. Say each phrase.*

**Stand up.**

**Go to the board.**

**Sit down.**

**Raise your hand.**

**Open your books.**

**Close your books.**

 **"Please Do It"**

*(reinforces commands)*

*Choose a leader.*

**Leader:**

*Give five commands from the vocabulary on page 34 to the class, one at a time.*

**Class:**

*Follow the leader's directions.*

**The Game:**

*Follow the leader's directions ONLY if the leader says "please."*

**Example:**  **Leader:**  "Stand up, please."
*or* "Please stand up."
(Class stands up.)

**Leader:**  "Stand up."
(Class *doesn't* stand up.)

**Leader** **Bonus** **Points:** *Use commands not on the vocabulary list on page 34.*

**Class** **Bonus** **Points:** *Help your classmates. Tell them, "Don't stand up!" if the leader doesn't say "please."*

> Stand up.

 **Listening with a Purpose**

**Focus Attention 1**

🎧 *Listen to the telephone voice mail message.*

| | | | |
|---|---|---|---|
| leave | message | Jim | Jack |
| Toronto | Montreal | business group | tour group |
| Grandma | Grandpa | Billy | Alice |
| Nancy | Tuesday | Thursday | piano lesson |
| guitar lesson | brush their teeth | $1.65 | $1.75 |

🎧 *Now listen to the telephone message again. Circle the words and phrases you hear.*

🎧 *Now listen to some of the sentences again. Fill in the blanks.*

**1.** Please _____ a message after the tone.

**2.** To listen to _____ message, _____ one.

**3.** We're with _____ tour group this morning.

**4.** _____ forget to call Grandpa, OK?

**5.** And _____ sure they brush _____ teeth.

# **W**riting
## **Phone Messages**

🎧 *Listen to Joanne's voice mail. Leave her a message slip for each of her calls.*

| **Message** | **Message** | **Message** |
|---|---|---|
| CALLER .................... | CALLER .................... | CALLER .................... |
| FROM .................... | FROM .................... | FROM .................... |
| PHONE NUMBER .................... | PHONE NUMBER .................... | PHONE NUMBER .................... |
| MESSAGE .................... | MESSAGE .................... | MESSAGE .................... |

**Heart to Heart**

*I think...*  *In my opinion...*  *because...*

*Look at the pictures. Which things are good or useful for you or your family?*
*Which things are not good or useful for you or your family? Why? Talk with a partner.*
*Compare your opinions.*

*I feel...*
*I don't think...*
*What about you?*

**Warm up:** Talk about this picture with a partner.
• Ask questions about the picture. • Talk about the people.
• What are their relationships? • Where are they?
• What things are in the picture?

**Then:** Create conversations for the people. OR Tell a story about the picture. Say as much as you can.

# Unit 4

# What's Bob doing?

**W**arm up: Look at the pictures. Where are these people?
Read or listen. 🎧

## Comprehension: Confirming Content

*Mark the following statements **true**, **false**, or **I don't know.***

|  |  | True | False | I don't know. |
|---|---|:---:|:---:|:---:|
| **Example:** | George is making pizzas. | ☐ | ☑ | ☐ |
| **1.** | Bob is making pizzas. | ☐ | ☐ | ☐ |
| **2.** | Luigi's is a restaurant. | ☐ | ☐ | ☐ |
| **3.** | Mr. Richards is ordering pizza for lunch. | ☐ | ☐ | ☐ |
| **4.** | Jim and Ted are out. | ☐ | ☐ | ☐ |
| **5.** | Luigi is busy. | ☐ | ☐ | ☐ |

# HOW TO talk about actions in progress/apologize/offer to call back later

## The Present Continuous

Use the present continuous to talk about actions in progress now.

They**'re making** pizzas.

Form the present continuous with a form of **be** and a present participle.

$\overbrace{\quad}^{be}$ $\overbrace{\qquad}^{present\ participle}$
Bob   is   working.

Make negative statements with **not**.

I'm **not** working today.

Some statements in the present continuous describe activities over a period of time.

$\overbrace{\qquad\qquad}^{period\ of\ time\ in\ the\ present}$
We aren't driving to work this week.

**TIP:** How to use contractions in the present continuous:

Bob**'s** working today.

They **aren't** serving customers.

**GRAMMAR TASK:** Find sentences with the present continuous in the photo story on pages 38–39.

## Conversation

🎧 *Read and listen to the conversation.*

**A:** Hello?

**B:** Hi, Sue. This is Ed. Are you busy?

**A:** Well, I'm making lunch right now. I'm sorry. Can I call you back?

**B:** Sure. No problem.

**A:** Bye.

🎧 *Listen again and practice.*

## Vocabulary • Everyday Activities

🎧 *Look at the pictures. Say each word or phrase.*

**exercise**

**make dinner**

**do homework**

**watch TV**

**talk to a friend**

**work**

**play ball**

**fix the car**

## Pair Practice

*Practice the conversation and vocabulary with a partner. Use the vocabulary above and your own words.*

**A:** Hello?

**B:** Hi, _____. This is _____. Are you busy?

**A:** Well, I'm _____ right now. I'm sorry. Can I call you back?

**B:** Sure. No problem.

**A:** Bye.

☑ **Now you know how to apologize and offer to call someone back when you are busy.**

| The Present Continuous: Questions | |
|---|---|
| ***yes-no* questions** | **possible answers** |
| Are you doing your homework? | No, I'm not doing it now. |
| Is he making dinner? | Yes, he is. |

**TIP:** Short answers to ***yes-no*** questions in the present continuous are the same as for ***be***.
　　　Are you studying? **Yes, I am.**

| ***wh-* questions** | **possible answers** |
|---|---|
| Who's teaching this class? | Mr. Young is. |
| What are you doing? | Watching TV. |
| Where are you working? | In my room. |

▼ **GRAMMAR TASK:** Answer the same questions in your own words.

## Grammar and Vocabulary in a Context

*Look at each picture. Complete the telephone conversations with forms of the present continuous.*

Hi, Mandy. What _____?
**1.** you / do

_____ TV. It's a mystery story.
**2.** I / watch
It's really exciting. Can I call you back later?

Hi, Dad. How are the kids? _____?
**3.** they / sleep

No, honey. _____
**4.** They / play
outside with the other kids.

But Dad, it's nine-thirty in the evening!

Yes, but remember—there's no school tomorrow.
_____ a good time. They're OK.
**5.** They / have

Pete, is Luigi there?

I'm sorry, Mrs. Moreno. He's not here right now.

_____ a pizza?
**6.** he / deliver

I don't know where he is. Sorry.

How's the weather there, Marsha? _____?
**7.** It / rain

No, _____.
**8.** it / snow

Snowing? In April? That's too bad. It's beautiful here. _____.
**9.** The sun / shine

## Grammar with a Partner

*With a partner, write questions in the present continuous about the photo story on pages 38–39.*

**Example:** Who's talking on the phone?

☑ **Now you know how to talk about actions in progress.**

In Your Own Words

**Look at the picture on page 49. Make negative statements. (Example: "The girl is not talking on the telephone.")**

# Listening with a Purpose

## Determine Context

🎧 *Listen to the telephone conversation. Make notes on this chart.*

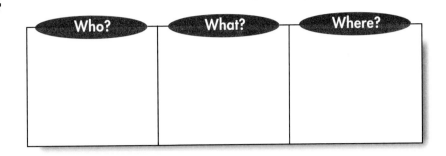

| Who? | What? | Where? |
|------|-------|--------|
|      |       |        |

*Now circle the correct letter.*

**1.** Who is calling Luigi?

   **a.** Bob is.     **b.** George is.     **c.** Bob's dad is.

**2.** What is the problem?

   **a.** He's late.     **b.** He's scared.     **c.** He's busy.

**3.** Why?

   **a.** He's stuck in traffic.     **b.** He's busy.     **c.** He's studying.

**4.** How is he getting to the restaurant?

   **a.** He's driving.     **b.** He's walking.     **c.** He's delivering a pizza.

**5.** Where is he calling from?

   **a.** He's calling from his home phone.     **b.** He's calling from the pizzeria.     **c.** He's calling from a car.

### SOCIAL LANGUAGE AND GRAMMAR 2
# How to give directions to a place/talk about order

## Conversation

🎧 *Read and listen to the conversation.*

**A:** Hello?

**B:** Vicky, we're late. I'm sorry. We're lost.

**A:** Well, where are you calling from?

**B:** Uh, let's see. We're at the corner of Lincoln Avenue and Seventh Street.

**A:** OK. Go down Lincoln Avenue to the second light. Then turn left. We're the first house on the right. You can't miss it.

🎧 *Listen again and practice.*

Lincoln    Avenue

Seventh Street    Eighth Street    Ninth Street

Wilson    Avenue

Washington    Avenue

★ = Public Phone

📱 = Light (Traffic Light)

## Vocabulary • Ordinal Numbers 1–12

🎧 *Look at the pictures. Say each word.*

FIRST · SECOND · THIRD · FOURTH · FIFTH · SIXTH · SEVENTH · EIGHTH · NINTH · TENTH · ELEVENTH · TWELFTH

## Pair Practice

*Practice the conversation and vocabulary with a partner. Use your own words.*

**A:** Hello?

**B:** _____, _____ late. I'm sorry. _____ lost.

**A:** Well, where are you calling from?

**B:** Uh, let's see. We're at the corner of _____ and _____.

**A:** OK. Go down _____ to the _____. Then turn _____. We're the _____ house on the right. You can't miss it.

☑ **Now you know how to give directions to a place.**

**Improvise**

*Look at the picture on page 49. Improvise a telephone conversation for the man and the woman. The woman apologizes. The man tells her what everyone in the room is doing.*

**Heart to Heart**

*I think...*
*In my opinion...*    *because...*

*With a partner, talk about lateness. Compare your opinions.*

Are some people always late?
When a friend is late, is that OK?

*I feel...*    *I don't think...*
*What about you?*

# Lost in Cascadia

*(reinforces asking for and giving directions)*

Look at this map of downtown Cascadia.
Work with a partner.

*Partner B, look at page 144.*

*Partner A, you are lost in Cascadia. You want to go to one of these places:*

Radio Shack
Farmers' Market
Cascadia Art Museum
Music Villa
Chong's Chinese Restaurant
Antoine's Fabulous French
   Restaurant
Pink Lotus Thai Restaurant
U.S. Post Office
Anita's Mexican Kitchen
Marvin's Department Store
Cineplex 12

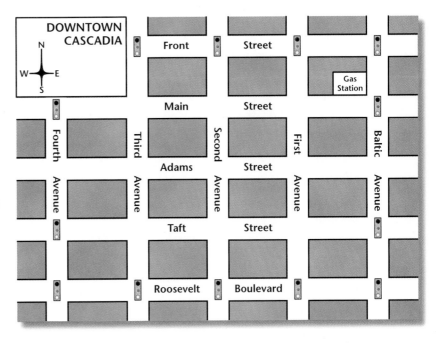

*You stop at the gas station at the corner of Baltic Avenue and Main Street and use the public phone. Your friend, Partner B, lives in Cascadia.*

*Call your friend and ask for directions. Then write the name of the place on your map. Use the following locations and directions.*

## Vocabulary • Locations and Directions

🎧 *Read and listen to these sentences.*

**Go down** Main Street **to** Third Avenue.

It's **at the corner of** Main Street **and** Third Avenue.

**Turn left.**

**Turn right.**

It's **between** First Avenue **and** Second Avenue.

**Example:**   **A:** Hello, _____? This is _____. I'm a little lost. I'm going
                   to the Farmers' Market. Right now I'm at a gas station at the
                   corner of Baltic Avenue and Main Street.

              **B:** No problem. Go down _____ to . . .

*Switch roles and maps with Partner B. Now you give the directions.*

# **H**OW TO **talk about actions in progress (more practice)**

Read these sentences in the present continuous. Look at the subject and object pronouns.

subject pronoun     object pronoun

She's    calling    **him.**

subject pronoun           object pronoun

I'm   working with   **her**   at the restaurant.

| object pronouns | |
|---|---|
| me | us |
| him | you |
| her | them |
| it | |

**GRAMMAR TASK:** Look at the "First Day on the Job" conversation on page 47. Find and underline an object pronoun in it.

## **Grammar in a Context**

*Complete the conversations with the correct object pronouns.*

**1. Man:** Jimmy, I'm fixing the car. Can you help _____?
                                          **1.**

    **Teenager:** Sorry, I'm busy. But Sarah's not busy. Ask _____.
                                                   **2.**

**2. First man:** Is Adam waiting for you?

    **Second man:** Yes, I'm meeting _____ in front of the theater.
                                               **3.**

**3. Woman:** Is that a good TV show?

    **Young girl:** Yes. Come and watch _____.
                                           **4.**

**4. Boy:** Sue and I are playing Monopoly. Play with _____, Mom. Please?
                                                     **5.**

    **Woman:** I'm busy. How about Dad and Will? Ask _____ to play with _____.
                                                 **6.**                                **7.**

# Reading

## A Conversation with an Inventor

# First Day on the Job

**B**efore You Read: *Talk about this picture.*
*Read the conversation.* 🎧

Dr. Dean is a professor and an inventor.
Amy Lane is Dr. Dean's new assistant.

**Dr. Dean:** OK, Amy. Here's your desk. And
this is your computer.

**Amy:** Oh, it's nice. Thanks. Wow!
What's that on your lab table?

**Dr. Dean:** It's my invention. I'm still
working on it.

**Amy:** Who are those people?

**Dr. Dean:** They're students. Right now you're looking at a history class.
Look. The teacher is writing a date on the board.

**Amy:** Oh, it's a security system.

**Dr. Dean:** No, it isn't. And it's not electrical. It's similar to a crystal ball.

**Amy:** A crystal ball? You're kidding. That's magic.

**Dr. Dean:** No, Amy, it's not. It's real. Test it. Give me a name and a location.

**Amy:** How about Bob Mercer at Luigi's? He's working there right now.

**Dr. Dean:** Perfect. Look.

**Amy:** That's incredible. There he is. And he's making a pizza, too. Wow!
What a fantastic invention!

## **C**omprehension: Drawing Conclusions

*Mark the following statements **true** or **false**.*

|  | True | False |
|---|:---:|:---:|
| **1.** Amy is Dr. Dean's assistant. | ☐ | ☐ |
| **2.** Dr. Dean's invention is a security system. | ☐ | ☐ |
| **3.** Dr. Dean and Amy are in a history classroom. | ☐ | ☐ |

*What do you think? Is this story possible?*

# Writing

## A Letter About What You Are Doing Now

*Imagine you are a student with Dr. Dean's invention. It's nighttime. You are looking at someone or something right now.*

*Write a friend about it. In your letter, answer these questions about what you are watching: What is it? or Who is it? Where is the person or thing you are watching? What is that person doing? Where are you?*

*Remember to begin your letter with "Dear" and your friend's name. Use a comma. Put the month and the day at the top of the letter.*

May 26
Dear Kevin,

Right now I'm sitting in my room. I'm using a wonderful new invention. It's fantastic. I'm watching the people in the pizzeria on the corner of Lexington Avenue and Third Street. Frank is making a pizza. He's talking to Anne. She's eating a pizza. This invention is not a camera. It's like magic. Incredible.

Talk to you soon.

Jane

# Pronunciation

/iʸ/ and /ɪ/

🎧 *Listen to these words.*

| /iʸ/ | sleep | please | Dean | study | leave |
|---|---|---|---|---|---|
| /ɪ/ | it | Jim | is | sit | live |

🎧 *Listen again and repeat.*

🎧 *Listen to the words and place a check mark in the box of the sound you hear.*

I'm **living** in an apartment on Baltic Avenue now.

I'm **leaving** for work now. Talk to you later.

| | /iʸ/ | /ɪ/ |
|---|---|---|
| **1.** him | ☐ | ☐ |
| **2.** teach | ☐ | ☐ |
| **3.** isn't | ☐ | ☐ |
| **4.** this | ☐ | ☐ |
| **5.** she | ☐ | ☐ |
| **6.** these | ☐ | ☐ |
| **7.** pizza | ☐ | ☐ |
| **8.** he | ☐ | ☐ |
| **9.** cheese | ☐ | ☐ |

*Now read the words out loud.*

**W**arm up: Talk about this picture with a partner. • Ask each other questions. • Talk about the people. • What are their relationships? • What time is it? • What is their address? • Where are these people? • Talk about what each person is doing. • Talk about the things and rooms in the house.

**T**hen: Create conversations for the people. OR Tell a story about the picture. Say as much as you can.

# You lose it. We find it.

**W**arm up: Look at the first picture. What are the partners' names? Listen.

Percy Brand
1940-1988
Beloved
Husband
of Doris

6

7

Welcome to Computer class!

8

## Comprehension: Confirming Content

*Now listen to "You lose it. We find It." again. Mark the following statements **true**, **false**, or **I don't know.***

|  |  | True | False | I don't know. |
|---|---|:---:|:---:|:---:|
| **Example:** | Sam is a detective. | ☑ | ☐ | ☐ |
| **1.** | Sam is married. | ☐ | ☐ | ☐ |
| **2.** | Doris has children. | ☐ | ☐ | ☐ |
| **3.** | Doris loves her work. | ☐ | ☐ | ☐ |
| **4.** | Sam is a student. | ☐ | ☐ | ☐ |
| **5.** | Doris works in two places. | ☐ | ☐ | ☐ |

# **H**OW TO **talk about work/ask about and express likes**

## The Simple Present Tense

**statements**

Use the simple present tense to state facts and describe habitual actions.

> Many Americans **work** part-time. (fact)
>
> Judy **swims** three times a week. (habitual action)

In the simple present tense, use the base form of the verb with **I, you, we,** and **they**.

> I **work** part-time.

Use the base form + **-s** or **-es** with **he, she,** and **it.**

> Doris **works** part-time, too.

**GRAMMAR TASK:** Look at this sentence. Is it a habitual action or an action in progress?

> Sam is working at home tonight.

**TIP:** Remember to use the present continuous to talk about actions in progress now.

> What's Doris doing? She's **talking** to Sam.

| *yes-no* questions | possible answers |
|---|---|
| Does he work with her? | Yes, he does. |
| Does she have a new computer? | No, she doesn't. |
| Sam, do I need a detective? | Yes, you do. |
| Do you work here? | Yes, I do. |
| Do they work with the detectives? | No, they don't. |

**GRAMMAR TASK:** Find a *yes-no* question in the conversation below.

## Conversation

🎧 *Read and listen to the conversation.*

**A:** Do you work?

**B:** Mm-hmm. I work part-time in a doctor's office—
from three to five.

**A:** Oh. Do you like it?

**B:** Yes, I do. I like it a lot.

🎧 *Listen again and practice.*

## Vocabulary • Places to Work

🎧 *Look at the pictures. Say each word.*

**a restaurant**　　　　**an office**　　　　**a store**　　　　**a supermarket**

## Pair Practice

*Practice the conversation and vocabulary with a partner. Use your own words.*

**A:** Do you work?

**B:** Mm-hmm. I work part-time in _____—from _____.

**A:** Oh. Do you like it?

**B:** Yes, I do. I like it a lot.

☑ **Now you know how to talk about work and express likes.**

**In Your Own Words** — **Look at the picture on page 61. Ask a partner a *yes-no* question about the picture. Use *Do* or *Does* and your own words.**

SOCIAL LANGUAGE AND GRAMMAR 2

# **H**OW TO ask about studies/express dislikes

## Vocabulary • Fields of Study

🎧 *Look at the pictures. Say each word.*

**math**　　**art**　　**medicine**　　**music**　　**dance**　　**journalism**　　**computers**　　**business**

| The Simple Present Tense | |
|---|---|
| ***wh-* questions** | **possible answers** |
| Who studies law? | Sam does. |
| What does Mary teach? | This class. |
| When do you go to class? | From ten to three. |

## Conversation

🎧 *Read and listen to the conversation.*

**A:** Do you study full-time?

**B:** No, I don't. I'm only taking two classes. What about you?

**A:** I study full-time at the university.

**B:** Oh. What do you study?

**A:** Drama.

**B:** Really? I bet that's fun. Do you like it?

**A:** No, not really.

🎧 *Listen again and practice.*

## Vocabulary • Some Adjectives to Describe Studies

🎧 *Read and listen to these words.*

| interesting | easy | fun | exciting | boring | hard | difficult |
|---|---|---|---|---|---|---|

## Pair Practice

*Practice the conversation and vocabulary with a partner. Use your own words.*

**A:** Do you study full-time?

**B:** No, I don't. I'm only taking _____. What about you?

**A:** _____.

**B:** Oh. What _____?

**A:** _____.

**B:** Really? I bet that's _____. Do you like it?

**A:** _____.

☑ **Now you know how to ask about studies. And you know how to say you don't like something.**

**Look at the picture on page 61. With a partner, create a conversation for the tall man and the short woman. Use your own words.**

## Improvise

*Work with a partner. Talk about your activities outside of class. Ask a lot of questions. Then tell the class about your partner. Say as much as you can.*

**Example:**  Do you work? Where do you work? etc.

**Then:**  _____ works full-time. He likes his work. He works in a bank, etc.

# How to **talk about habitual activities (more practice)**

## Grammar in a Context

🎧 *Listen to these sentences about the detectives. Then complete them by choosing the verb you hear.*

**1.** Sam Armstrong _____ his work.
<u>loves / love</u>

**2.** He _____ missing people.
<u>finds / find</u>

**3.** He _____ information.
<u>gets / get</u>

**4.** Doris Brand _____ with Sam.
<u>works / work</u>

**5.** She _____ her partner.
<u>likes / like</u>

**6.** Sam and Doris _____ a detective agency.
<u>has / have</u>

**7.** Sam _____ law in the evenings.
<u>studies / study</u>

**8.** Doris _____ part-time.
<u>teach / teaches</u>

---

**The Simple Present Tense: Spelling the Third-Person Form**

If the base form ends in **sh, ch, x, s, z,** or **o,** add **-es:** tea**ch** / teach**es**

If the base form ends in a consonant plus **y,** change the **y** to **i** and add **-es:** worr**y** / worr**ies**

If the base form ends in any other letter, add **-s:** liv**e** / live**s**

**TIP:** The verb **have** is an exception: **have / has**

# Reading

## A Business Consultation with Detectives

***Before You Read:*** *Who are Sam and Doris? What is their occupation?*

*Read the conversation.* 🎧

# A Day in the Life of a Detective

**Doris:** OK, Mr. and Mrs. Mason. How can we help you?

**Mrs. Mason:** It's about our son Joe.

**Sam:** What about him? We're detectives. Is he missing or something?

**Mrs. Mason:** No, he's not missing. But some days he doesn't go to school.

**Doris:** Where's he spending the day?

**Mr. Mason:** That's what we want to know. Sometimes we follow him. But when we follow him, he always goes to school.

**Mrs. Mason:** Sometimes he goes to school every day for a month, but then he doesn't go for a day or two. We're worried.

**Sam:** Yes, you need a detective. It's impossible for you to follow him every day. That's a detective's job.

**Doris:** Do you have a recent picture of Joe?

**Mrs. Mason:** Yes, we do. Here it is.

**Sam:** How tall is he? What color is his hair? How old is he?

**Mr. Mason:** He has reddish curly hair. He's six feet tall. He's sixteen. And he always wears a green baseball cap.

**Doris:** What about his likes and dislikes?

**Mrs. Mason:** Well, he loves pizza . . . and fast food . . . and animals.

## Comprehension: Identifying the Main Idea

*Choose another title for "A Day in the Life of a Detective."*

**a.** Joe Mason at School

**b.** A Problem for the Masons

# Writing

## A Detective's Notes

*Sam and Doris keep notes of all their cases. Write notes on the Mason case for them.*

**Sam Armstrong • Doris Brand**
**Private Investigators**

You lose it. We find it.

**Case Notes**

**Case:** Sophie Miller

**Problem:** Car is missing

**Physical Description:** Black 1998 Toyota

**Other Information:** She works at Acme Shoe Factory. She parks the car in the company parking lot every day.

**Sam Armstrong • Doris Brand**
**Private Investigators**

You lose it. We find it.

**Case Notes**

**Case:**

**Problem:**

**Physical Description:**

**Other Information:**

*Receptive Model*

# Listening with a Purpose

## Determine Context

🎧 *Listen to the conversation. Make notes on this chart as you listen.*

| Who? | What? |
| --- | --- |
|  |  |

*Circle the correct letter.*

**1.** Who has a problem?

   **a.** Sam and Doris      **b.** Mr. and Mrs. Foley

**2.** The conversation is about _____.

   **a.** a missing person      **b.** a missing animal

## Focus Attention

🎧 *Look at this picture. Listen to the conversation again. This time, listen specifically for names. Then write the name of each person and animal you hear about in the conversation.*

SOCIAL LANGUAGE AND GRAMMAR 4

# How to talk about likes and dislikes/describe habitual activities (more practice)

### The Simple Present Tense: Negative

Form the negative of *I, we, you,* and *they* with *don't* + the base form of the verb.

> I *don't like* pizza, but I love cheese.

Form the negative of *he, she,* and *it* with *doesn't* + the base form of the verb.

> Doris *doesn't have* a son.

**TIP:** The uncontracted forms (*do not* and *does not*) make negative statements stronger.

**GRAMMAR TASK:** Find and underline sentences with negative forms of the simple present tense in the reading on page 56.

**Look at the picture on page 61. With a partner, write as many sentences in your own words as you can about this picture in one minute. Which pair of students writes the most sentences?**

# Be a Detective

*(reinforces questions in the simple present tense)*

*Walk around your classroom for three minutes. Find people who fit these categories. Ask questions. Get each person's initials.*

**Example:**  Do you eat breakfast?

| POINTS FOR EACH THING | FIND SOMEONE WHO | PERSON'S INITIALS | YOUR SCORE |
|---|---|---|---|
| 2 | doesn't eat breakfast | J.S. | 2 |
| 2 | hates spiders | L.M. | 4 |
| 4 | doesn't live in a house | | |
| 8 | speaks German | | |
| 10 | likes to eat snails | | |
| 1 | eats at fast-food restaurants | | |
| 7 | doesn't like rock music | | |
| 10 | likes snakes | | |
| 6 | has an unusual pet (not a cat or dog) | | |
| 8 | hates sports | | |
| 3 | wears contact lenses | | |
| 8 | doesn't like fast food | | |
| 9 | studies ballet | | |
| 7 | likes opera | | |
| 5 | worries a lot | | |
| 6 | has a coin with a date before 1990 | | |
| 8 | doesn't drink coffee | | |
| 9 | doesn't eat meat | | |

your total score _____

*Use the chart and talk about your classmates' likes and dislikes.*

## Heart to Heart

Compare your likes and dislikes with a partner's. Compare your favorite things.

Talk about these categories.

| TV programs | kinds of music | places |
|---|---|---|
| activities | foods | kinds of people |

*I think...*

*In my opinion...*

*because...*

*I feel...*

*I don't think...*

*What about you?*

## Pronunciation
### /s/, /z/, /ɪz/

🎧 Read and listen to the following verbs.

| ends in an /s/ sound | | ends in a /z/ sound | | ends in an /ɪz/ sound | |
|---|---|---|---|---|---|
| write | writes | run | runs | wash | washes |
| make | makes | love | loves | watch | watches |
| like | likes | study | studies | teach | teaches |

🎧 Listen again and repeat.

🎧 Now listen to the following verbs and write them in the correct columns, according to the sound you hear.

| ends in an /s/ sound | ends in a /z/ sound | ends in an /ɪz/ sound |
|---|---|---|
| _____ | _____ | _____ |
| _____ | _____ | _____ |
| _____ | _____ | _____ |
| _____ | _____ | _____ |

**Warm up:** Talk about this picture with a partner.
• Where is this? • Talk about the people in the picture.
• What are they doing? • What are they saying?
• Who is at the window? • What do you see in the picture?

**Then:** Create conversations for the people. OR Tell a story about the picture. Say as much as you can.

# Review, SelfTest, and Extra Practice

## Part 1

### Review

## Computer Class

🎧 *Read or listen to this conversation in a computer class.*

Doris Brand is the teacher. Steve and Alice are her students.

**Doris:** Hi, everybody. Welcome back. Ready? OK. Here we go. Please turn on your computers first. OK. Now is everyone in File Manager?

**Steve:** Uh-oh. This is really different! All my training is on the Mac.

**Alice:** Don't worry. It's not that hard.

**Steve:** Are you pretty advanced at this stuff?

**Alice:** Not really. Photography is my hobby, so I'm here to learn computer graphics.

**Doris:** Steve, do you need help?

**Steve:** Well . . . yes, I do. I'm new to the PC, and I'm not a computer genius.

**Doris:** Just treat it like the Mac. It's pretty similar.

**Alice:** Really. Don't worry. Let's talk after class.

**Steve:** Great. Thanks.

## SelfTest

### Comprehension: Confirming Content

🎧 *Read or listen again to the conversation in Doris's computer class.*
*Then mark the following statements **true**, **false**, or **I don't know**.*

| | | True | False | I don't know. |
|---|---|:---:|:---:|:---:|
| **Example:** | Doris's class is an English class. | ☐ | ☑ | ☐ |
| **1.** | Doris teaches a computer class. | ☐ | ☐ | ☐ |
| **2.** | Steve has a Mac at home. | ☐ | ☐ | ☐ |
| **3.** | Alice wants to learn computer graphics. | ☐ | ☐ | ☐ |
| **4.** | Alice is married. | ☐ | ☐ | ☐ |
| **5.** | Steve is a computer genius. | ☐ | ☐ | ☐ |

### Improvise

With a partner, pretend you are students in a computer class
(or another kind of class: art, cooking, photography, etc.).
One student is worried. The other student wants to help.
Have a conversation.

*Extra Practice*

## Part 2

### Review

## An Invitation

🎧 *Listen to Steve and Alice's*
*conversation after class.*

## **G**rammar: Verb Review

🎧 *Listen again to Steve and Alice's conversation after class. Fill in the blanks with the correct pronouns and verb forms. Remember to use a capital letter if a word begins a sentence.*

**Alice:** Well, Steve. _____ me about yourself. What do you do?
　　　　　　　　　　　**1.**

**Steve:** Well, _____ see. _____ a student here at the college.
　　　　　　　　**2.**　　　　　**3.**

　　　　Uh . . . I _____ soccer for the college, too.
　　　　　　　　**4.**

**Alice:** Soccer? _____ great. I _____ soccer. And what _____ you _____?
　　　　　　　　　**5.**　　　　　　**6.**　　　　　　　　**7.**　　　　　**8.**

**Steve:** Physical education. I _____ sports.
　　　　　　　　　　　　　　**9.**

**Alice:** _____ you _____ with friends?
　　　　**10.**　　　　　**11.**

**Steve:** Uh, no, I _____. I _____ alone.
　　　　　　　　**12.**　　　　**13.**

**Alice:** _____ you _____ the college?
　　　　**14.**　　　　　**15.**

**Steve:** Well, _____ OK. But my business classes _____ really
　　　　　　　**16.**　　　　　　　　　　　　　　**17.**

　　　　hard. I have to work with spreadsheets and data bases. I really

　　　　_____ about that. And now this class _____ a different computer.
　　　　**18.**　　　　　　　　　　　　　　**19.**

**Alice:** I _____ an idea. Why _____ you _____ to my house
　　　　**20.**　　　　　　**21.**　　　　**22.**

　　　　tomorrow and meet my grandson? _____ a computer whiz.
　　　　　　　　　　　　　　　　　**23.**

**Steve:** Oh . . . no, I . . . uh . . . have to study.

**Alice:** Oh come on. Tomorrow night at seven-thirty? 610 13th Avenue.

**Steve:** _____ you sure?
　　　　**24.**

**Alice:** Of course. See you tomorrow evening.

**Steve:** Thanks a lot.

## Pair Practice

*Talk with a partner about work and studies. Use this conversation as a guide.*

**A:** Do you _____? (work/study)

**B:** _____.

**A:** I bet that's _____.

**B:** _____. What about you?

**A:** _____.

**B:** Do you like it?

**A:** _____.

# Part 3

## Review

# New Friends

🎧 *Read or listen to the conversation at Alice's house the next day.*

Hi, Steve. Come on in.

This is my grandson Charlie. Charlie, this is Steve.

Hi, Steve.

Hi. Nice to meet you.

And this is my friend Julie.

Hi, Steve. Are you a computer addict like Charlie?

No, not really. But I'm learning. I'm taking a course. That's how I know Alice.

Oh, cool. Do you go to the college?

Yeah, I do. What about you?

## SelfTest

### Comprehension: Factual Recall

*Circle the correct letter.*

**1.** Who is Charlie?

    **a.** Steve's friend      **b.** Alice's grandson      **c.** Julie's grandson

**2.** Who is Julie?

    **a.** Alice's granddaughter      **b.** Steve's friend      **c.** Charlie's friend

**3.** Where are these people talking to each other?

    **a.** in Doris's computer class      **b.** in Alice's house      **c.** at the college

**4.** What does Charlie love?

    **a.** computers      **b.** the college      **c.** physical education

**5.** What does Julie study at the college?

    **a.** French      **b.** physical education      **c.** computers

**Extra Practice**

### Improvise

*Work with a partner. Review the conversations on pages 62 and 64. Then improvise a similar conversation, asking each other about activities outside of class. Finish by inviting your partner to do something with you or suggesting some place to go.*

### Vocabulary: Parts of the Computer

the printer

the screen

an icon

the mouse

the keyboard

## Space Invaders

*First look at the computer vocabulary above. Then read or listen to Steve and Charlie's conversation after dinner.*

**Charlie:** I've got a great idea. Let's play a game on my PC. Maybe it sounds silly, but it's a great way for you to learn the PC.

**Steve:** What about Space Invaders? I know that one. My little sister plays it all the time. Do you have that?

**Charlie:** Hmm. Yeah, I do. . . . OK, Steve. You're in the driver's seat. You take the mouse.

**Steve:** OK. Here we go.

**Charlie:** All right. Now select that icon.

**Steve:** Cool. That's Zorgon. How do I select it?

**Charlie:** The same as on the Mac. Click on it.

**Steve:** OK. What's next?

**Charlie:** Simple. You zap the invaders. Like this.

**Steve:** My sister isn't going to believe this—her big brother playing Space Invaders.

**Charlie:** Steve, watch out! There are the invaders! Oh no! Too late. Zorgon's dead.

**Steve:** Oh well. Too bad. Maybe next time. Want to play again?

## Grammar: Definite and Indefinite Articles: *a, an, the*

*Read the conversation about Space Invaders on page 67. Use the information in that conversation to complete this paragraph with **a, an, the,** or no article.*

Steve and Charlie are in Charlie's room, playing _____ computer games.
1.

Space Invaders is _____ computer game. It's _____ fun. When you play
2.                                    3.

Space Invaders, you click on _____ zoom box to maximize _____ screen.
4.                                        5.

Zorgon is _____ hero. He fights with _____ invaders. Sometimes
6.                                7.

_____ invaders win. Sometimes _____ Zorgon wins.
8.                                        9.

**Extra Practice**

# Writing
### Describing a Game

*Describe Space Invaders or your favorite computer game. Use the conversation on page 67 as a model.*

## Part 5

## Review

# Technology in Our Lives

Are you afraid of technology? Is technology a good thing? Many Americans think so. In the United States, about 90 percent of families have television. About 99 percent of the 90 percent have color TV. About 79 percent have a VCR. Almost 40 percent have a computer. Many people have CD players. Many people have a vacuum cleaner, a washing machine, and a dryer.

But not everyone loves technology. Mrs. Amanda Titus of Dallas, Texas, doesn't like it at all. She says, "I hate modern inventions. They control our lives. I have a remote for my TV, and I don't know how to use it. My daughter watches TV all the time. She doesn't talk to me. My son plays computer games constantly. He doesn't do his homework. I'm afraid of technology. It controls our lives."

What do you think?

## Reading Comprehension: Factual Recall

*Complete the answers to items 1, 2, and 3. Then provide reasons for item 4.*

**1.** _____ percent of American homes have television.

**2.** _____ percent of American homes have a VCR.

**3.** Many Americans have _____, _____, and _____.

**4.** What are three reasons Mrs. Amanda Titus doesn't like technology?

    **a.** _____

    **b.** _____

    **c.** _____

*I think...*
*In my opinion...*
*because...*
*I feel...*
*I don't think...*
*What about you?*

**Extra Practice**

*Talk to a partner. Compare your opinions. Do you agree or disagree with Amanda Titus? Give examples and reasons for your opinions.*

## SOCIAL LANGUAGE SelfTest

*Circle the appropriate statement or question to complete each of the following conversations.*

**1. A:** I'm Jeanette Young.

  **B:** _____

    **a.** Hi, I'm Susan Peters. Nice to meet you.    **c.** Nice to meet you, too.

    **b.** Yes, I am.    **d.** What's your name?

**2. A:** _____

  **B:** It's nice to meet you, too.

    **a.** What's your name?    **c.** I'm a nice teacher.

    **b.** It's nice to meet you.    **d.** She's a teacher.

**3. A:** What's his name?

   **B:** _____

   **a.** Bob Stettner.    **c.** My name's Mark Smith.

   **b.** Amy Carlson.    **d.** Who's he?

**4. A:** There's a great movie at the Lido.

   **B:** _____

   **a.** Really?    **c.** Seven o'clock.

   **b.** How are you?    **d.** Who's that?

**5. A:** See you there.

   **B:** _____

   **a.** What is it?    **c.** OK.

   **b.** Why?    **d.** There's a rock concert at the stadium.

**6. A:** Do you want to go?

   **B:** _____

   **a.** See you later.    **c.** Bye.

   **b.** I'm so excited.    **d.** Maybe. What time?

**7. A:** What's your name and address?

   **B:** _____

   **a.** Michael Harris. 33 Riverside Drive.    **c.** 238-5803.

   **b.** China King Restaurant.    **d.** Anything else?

**8. A:** _____

   **B:** No, let's not. I'm tired.

   **a.** How's it going?    **c.** Call Mario's. Their pizza's great.

   **b.** Don't hang up.    **d.** Do you want to go to the movies tonight?

**9. A:** Spell your last name, please.

    **B:** _____

       238-5803.                                 Frances Silva.

       A-M-E-S.                                  Don't worry.

**10. A:** What number are you calling from?

    **B:** _____

       Nice to meet you, too.                 422-6701.

       My son is very sick.                  1214 Elm Street.

**11. A:** _____

    **B:** My homework.

       Where are you calling from?         What are you doing?

       Do you work here?                   Who's that?

**12. A:** Do you work?

    **B:** _____

       I like it a lot.                       He works from 10 to 3.

       No, I don't.                        In a doctor's office.

**13. A:** Do you like your job?

    **B:** _____

       I work part-time.                   He doesn't have a job.

       I study full-ime.                   Yes, I do.

**14. A:** I bet that's hard.

    **B:** _____

       Do you like it?                     No, I don't.

       How are you?                     Not really.

# Activity Links for 1A and 1B

## Unit 2

### Crazy Backwards Questions

*Partner B: Listen to Partner A's answers. When Partner A reads you an answer, read him or her a question from this list.*

How are these books?
Are you a student?
What time is it?
Where's the concert?
Who's the teacher?

*Now here is a list of five answers. Read each one to Partner A. Partner A gives you a question for each answer.*

That's the teacher.
No, there isn't.
I'm fine.
*Daughters of Dracula.*
No, he's single.

## Unit 4

### Lost in Cascadia

*Partner B: Partner A is lost and calls you for directions. Look at your map. Give Partner A directions.*

**Example:**
• • • • • •

**A:** Hello, _____? This is _____.
I'm a little lost. I'm going to the Cascadia Art Museum. Right now I'm at a gas station at the corner of Baltic Avenue and Main Street.

**B:** No problem. Go down _____ to . . .

*Switch roles with Partner A.
Get directions to another place.*

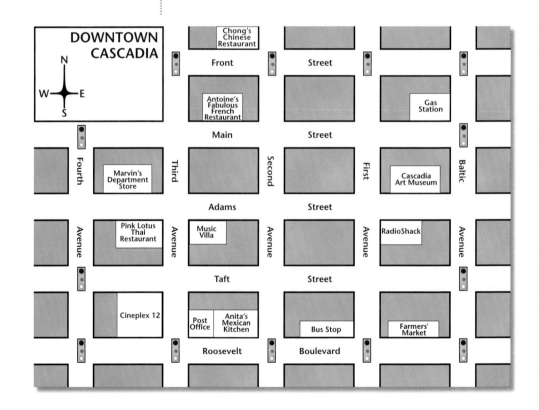

## Improvise

*Group B: Here are some items in the Men's Department. Tell Group A the prices of the things they want to buy. Have conversations.*

| | |
|---|---|
| bathing suit | $15 |
| belt | $12 |
| blue jeans | $24 |
| boxer shorts | $8 |
| briefs | $5 |
| dress shirt | $18 |
| pajamas | $15 |
| sport shirt | $12 |
| suit | $75 |
| sweater | $20 |
| tie | $16 |
| T-shirt | $10 |
| undershirt | $5 |

*Group C: Here are some items in the Women's Department. Tell Group A the prices of things they want to buy. Have conversations.*

| | |
|---|---|
| belt | $12 |
| bikini | $25 |
| blouse | $18 |
| bra | $12 |
| dress | $50 |
| nightgown | $15 |
| one-piece bathing suit | $25 |
| panty hose | $8 |
| panties | $8 |
| skirt | $30 |
| slacks | $50 |

*Group D: Here are some items in the Shoe Department. Tell Group A the prices of things they want to buy. Have conversations.*

| | |
|---|---|
| boots | $100 |
| loafers | $36 |
| men's dress shoes | $80 |
| running shoes | $45 |
| sandals | $24 |
| slippers | $30 |
| women's dress shoes | $50 |

## To Tell the Truth

*Contestant A: Here is the information you need to answer the questions. (You are not telling the truth.)*

1. My name was John F. Kennedy.
2. I was born in 1898.
3. I had nine brothers and sisters.
4. I grew up in New York.
5. No, I could not.
6. No, I didn't.
7. Yes, I was vice president.
8. I was married two times.
9. We had one child.
10. I was president from 1956 to 1960.
11. I was old when I died.
12. I died in Miami.
13. Her name was Jessie.

*Contestant B: Here is the information you need to answer the questions. (You are telling the truth.)*

1. My name was John F. Kennedy.
2. I was born in 1917.
3. I had eight brothers and sisters.
4. I grew up in Massachusetts.
5. Yes, I could.
6. Yes, I did.
7. Yes, I was a senator.
8. I was married once.
9. We had two children.
10. I was president from 1961 to 1963.
11. I was young when I died.
12. I died in Dallas, Texas.
13. Her name was Jackie.

*Contestant C: Here is the information you need to answer the questions. (You are not telling the truth.)*

1. My name was John F. Kennedy.
2. I was born in 1910.
3. I had six brothers and sisters.
4. I grew up in Florida.
5. No, I could not.
6. No, I didn't.
7. Yes, I was a governor.
8. I was married three times.
9. We had four children.
10. I was president from 1965 to 1968.
11. I was old when I died.
12. I died in Boston.
13. Her name was Jenny.

vocabulary list shows key words and expressions presented for students' active
te or indefinite article is included to help students with usage.

### 1

**Nouns**

an adult
an animal
an artist
a character
a class
a doctor
an engineer
a friend
a homemaker
a human
a lawyer
a man
a manager
a name
a neighbor
a nurse
a party
a secretary
a student
a superhero

a teacher
a teenager
a woman

**Verb: *Be***

am
is
are

**Adjectives**

athletic
boring
easy
fictional
great
hard
historical
interesting
married
old
real
short

single
studious
tall
young

**Adverb**

not

**Articles**

a
an
the

**Subject Pronouns**

I
you
he
she
it
we
you
they

**Contractions**

he's
I'm
we're
you're
they're
she's
it isn't
she isn't
we aren't

***Wh-* words**

what's
who's

**Expressions**

Nice to meet you.
Nice to meet you, too.

### Unit 2

**Nouns**

the afternoon
a cat
a concert
the evening
maps
the morning
a movie
a play
the time

*Days of the Week*

Monday
Tuesday
Wednesday
Thursday

Friday
Saturday
Sunday

*Count and Non-count Nouns*

a car
a dog
an elephant
an orange

bread
milk
snow
water

**Verbs**

go
want

**Adjectives**

excited
fine
good
OK
terrific

**Adverbs**

maybe
today
tomorrow
tonight

***Wh-* words**

what
when
why

**Prepositions**

at
in
on

**Expressions**

How are you?
See you later.
See you there.
That's great.

**Other**

there is
there are
there's

## Unit 3

### Nouns

an address
a cassette player
a CD player
a computer
a fax machine
a laptop
a message
a play
a phone number
pizza
a restaurant
a remote
a TV
a walk

*Family Relationships*

a mother
a father
a grandmother
a grandfather
a daughter
a son
a sister
a brother
a husband
a wife
a grandson
a granddaughter

### Verbs

go (to a rock concert,
    for a walk)
hang (up)
order (to)
press
spell
walk
watch

*Commands
(Imperatives)*

*choose* a partner
*close* the door
*go* to the board
*open* your books
*raise* your hand
*sit* down
*stand* up

### Possessive Adjectives

my
your
his
her
its
our
their

### Adjectives

broken
hungry
late

### Adverbs

please
ready
really

### *Wh-* words

how

### Preposition

about

### Expressions

Good idea.
Let's go.
Let's not (go out).
No problem.

---

## Unit 4

### Nouns

a ball
a car
a corner
dinner
directions
exercise
a gas station
homework
a house
a light
lunch
work

### Verbs

call
can't
do
fix
give
make
miss
play
run
turn

*Present Continuous:
Present Participles*

calling
delivering
doing
driving
exercising
fixing
leaving
living
making
serving
talking
watching
working

### Adjectives

busy
late
lost
left
right
sorry

### Adverbs

later
left
right

### Ordinal Numbers

first
second
third
fourth
fifth
sixth
seventh
eighth
ninth
tenth
eleventh
twelfth

### Object Pronouns

me
you
him
her
it
us
them

## Unit 5

### Nouns

*Places to Work*

an office
a restaurant
a store
a supermarket

*Fields of Study*

art
business
computers
dance
journalism
math
medicine
music
a detective

### Verbs

*Simple Present Tense*

find/finds
get/gets
has/have
like/likes
love/loves
study/studies
teach/teaches
work/works
worry/worries

*Negative Form*

does not/doesn't
do not/ don't

### Adjectives

difficult
easy
exciting
fun
hard
impossible
interesting
missing

### Other

a lot

## Unit 6

### Nouns

an appointment
breakfast
a date
a dating service
help
a meeting
a patient
a problem
weekdays

*Nouns Describing Illness*

a backache
a cough
a fever
a headache
a sore throat
a toothache

*Parts of the Body*

an ankle
an arm
a back
an elbow
a hand
a knee
a shoulder
a wrist

*Sports*

baseball
basketball
soccer
tennis
volleyball

### Verbs

be going to
hurt
leave
need

### Adjectives

bored
dizzy
excited
nervous
tired
worried

### Adverbs of Frequency

always
occasionally
often
never
rarely
seldom
sometimes
usually

### Prepositions

at
from
in the
out of

### Expressions

Gosh.
Good bye.
Thank you.
You're welcome.

## Unit 7

### Nouns

a bank
a dance
evening
a minute

*Activities*

biking
dancing
fishing
hiking
Roller-blading
skateboarding
swimming

*Courses of Study*

calculus
chemistry
English
history

### Verbs

can/can't
dance
have, has, have to, has to
help
play

### Adjectives

hard
other

### Adverbs

earlier
later

### Expressions

Good idea.
Please?
Sorry.
Thanks a million.

## Unit 8

### Nouns

*Shopping and Clothing*

a bathing suit
a belt
a bikini
a blouse
boots
boxer shorts
a bra
briefs
clothing
a coat
a department store
a dress
a dress shirt
gloves
a jacket
loafers
the men's department
mittens
a nightgown
pajamas
panty hose
panties
pants
a raincoat
running shoes
sandals
shoes
shorts
a size
a skirt
sleepwear
slippers
socks
a sport shirt
a suit
a sweater
a tie
a T-shirt
an umbrella
an undershirt
underwear
a windbreaker
the women's
    department

### Colors

beige
black
brown
blue
gray
green
orange
pink
purple
red
white
yellow

### Adjectives

any
much
some
that
these
this
those

### Pronouns

one
ones

### Expressions

Excuse me.
How can I help you?
Right this way.
You're kidding!

## Unit 9

### Nouns

last week
last weekend
today
yesterday

*Social and Business
Relationships*

an assistant
the boss
a boyfriend
fiancé(e)s
a girlfriend
a husband
neighbors
a partner
roommates
a wife

### Adjectives

familiar

### Verbs

look
know
was
were
wasn't
weren't

### Possessive Pronouns

mine
yours
his
hers
ours
their

### Wh- words

where
why

### Expressions

by the way
Don't worry.
go Dutch
I can afford it.
I'm sorry about that.
It's not fair.
No way!
oops
That's OK.
would you like to

## Unit 10

### Nouns

candy
cookies
mail

### Adverb

back

### Verbs

did not
didn't
sound

*Regular Past Forms*

played
practiced
studied

*Irregular Past Forms*

came
did
felt
found
forgot
got
grew
had
heard
knew
made
met
said
saw
told
took
thought
went

### Past Time Expressions

a few days ago
a little while ago
last month
last week
twenty minutes ago
yesterday

### Expressions

Guess who?

## Simple Past Tense of Irregular Verbs

| Base Form | Simple Past | Base Form | Simple Past |
|-----------|-------------|-----------|-------------|
| be | was, were | leave | left |
| become | became | let | let |
| begin | began | lose | lost |
| break | broke | make | made |
| bring | brought | meet | met |
| buy | bought | put | put |
| can | could (for ability | quit | quit |
| catch | only) | read | read |
| choose | caught | ride | rode |
| come | chose | run | ran |
| cut | came | say | said |
| do | cut | see | saw |
| drink | did | sell | sold |
| drive | drank | send | sent |
| eat | drove | sing | sang |
| fall | ate | sit | sat |
| feel | fell | sleep | slept |
| fight | felt | speak | spoke |
| fly | fought | stand | stood |
| forget | flew | steal | stole |
| get | forgot | take | took |
| give | got | teach | taught |
| go | gave | tell | told |
| grow | went | think | thought |
| have | grew | throw | threw |
| hear | had | understand | understood |
| hold | heard | wake | woke, waked |
| hurt | held | win | won |
| keep | hurt | write | wrote |
| know | kept | | |
| | knew | | |

## Irregular Noun Plurals

| Singular Form | Plural Form | Singular Form | Plural Form |
|---------------|-------------|---------------|-------------|
| child | children | person | people |
| foot | feet | tooth | teeth |
| knife | knives | wife | wives |
| life | lives | woman | women |
| man | men | | |

## Spelling Rules for the Present Participle

If the base form ends in a silent *-e:* Drop the *-e* and add *-ing.*

> make   +  -ing  =  making

If the base form ends in a single vowel + a single consonant (except *w, x,* and *y*):
Double the consonant and add *-ing.*

> run   +  -ing  =  running
> mix   +  -ing  =  mixing

Add *-ing* to all other base forms

> sleep   +  -ing  =  sleeping
> wash   +  -ing  =  washing

# TRUE COLORS

## An EFL Course for Real Communication

**WORKBOOK 1A**

**JAY MAURER**
**IRENE E. SCHOENBERG**

Workbook by Angela Blackwell

Joan Saslow
Series Director

# Unit 1 — Are you in this class?

## 1 Complete the conversations.

*Fill in the blanks with words from the box. You can use some words more than once.*

| I'm | He's | She's | We're | They're | It's |
| --- | --- | --- | --- | --- | --- |

**1. A:** This is Bob. _____*He's*_____ my neighbor.

   **B:** Hi, Bob.

**2. A:** Where's Susan?

   **B:** _____ in the car.

**3. A:** Hi! _____ Alison.

   **B:** Nice to meet you, Alison.

**4. A:** I'm Kate, and this is Emma. _____ in this class.

   **B:** Hi. I'm Tom.

**5. A:** How old is Mike?

   **B:** _____ nine.

**6. A:** Where's the English class?

   **B:** _____ in room 208.

**7. A:** Who's that?

   **B:** Adela. _____ Ron's wife.

**8. A:** What do you do?

   **B:** _____ an engineer.

**9. A:** Where are your friends?

   **B:** _____ in New York.

## ❷ Write sentences.

*Look at the pictures. Write a sentence for each picture. Use words from the box.*

| a doctor    a secretary    an engineer    a nurse    a lawyer    a homemaker |

**1.** ___He's an engineer.___

**2.** _____

**3.** _____

**4.** _____

**5.** _____

**6.** _____

## ❸ Unscramble the conversation.

*Put the conversation in the correct order.*

_____    So what do you do, Sally?

___1___    Sally, this is my friend Steve.

_____    I'm an engineer.

_____    Hi, Sally. Nice to meet you.

_____    I'm a teacher. What about you?

_____    Nice to meet you, too.

# 4 Write about yourself.

*Answer the questions. Tell about yourself. Use short answers.*

**Example:**  Are you tall?  _Yes, I am._____

1. Are you short?  _____

2. Are you a teenager?  _____

3. Are you a student?  _____

4. Are you single?  _____

5. Are you from the United States?  _____

6. Are you married?  _____

7. Are you athletic?  _____

8. Are you studious?  _____

# 5 Complete the sentences.

*Fill in the blanks with **a, an,** or **the.***

1. Sandra is _____a_____ doctor.

2. ____The____ doctor's name is Felix Yamamoto.

3. Carlos is _____ student at San Fernando College.

4. _____ students in my class are all very nice.

5. He's a nurse? But he's _____ man!

6. _____ new teacher is very young.

7. My friend is _____ artist. He's very good.

8. That's a beautiful picture. _____ artist is Paul Cummings.

9. I live in _____ United States.

## 6 Match descriptions and pictures.

*Look at the pictures. Match each sentence to the correct picture. Write the correct letter in the blank.*

**a.** They're good friends.     **b.** They're married.     **c.** She's studious.

**1.** _____     **2.** _____     **3.** _____

*Challenge*

## 7 Read and answer questions.

*Read the postcard.*
*Then write the correct answer in the blank.*

**1.** The postcard is to _____Danny_____.
   Jeff / Mexico / Danny

**2.** The postcard is from _____.
   Danny / Danny's teacher / Danny's mother

**3.** Danny lives in

   _____.
   Los Angeles / Berkeley / Mexico

**4.** Danny is

   _____.
   a student / a lawyer / a doctor

Beach     Ruins

Hi there!
    Mexico is beautiful!
Our hotel is really nice. The
people are friendly, and the
old Mayan ruins are
fascinating. And we love the
beaches! See you on the 17th.
Good luck with your classes!
    Love,
    Mom

March 10, 20--

Danny Leaver
1313 Washington Street, # B
Berkeley, CA 94703

# ⑧ Write addresses.

*Write the addresses on the envelopes. Pay attention to capital letters.*

Note: Illinois = IL   California = CA   Ohio = OH

**1.** john henry / 2034 rutherford road / champaign il 61821 / usa

**2.** andrea martin / 140 mission drive / arcadia ca 91006

**3.** alan mansell / personnel department / worldnet, inc. / 2000 arlington street / columbus oh 43220

# There's a noise downstairs!

## ❶ Circle the correct time.

*Look at the clocks. Circle the correct choice.*

**1. (a.)** It's four o'clock.

   **b.** It's a quarter to four.

**2. a.** It's three-fifteen.

   **b.** It's three forty-five.

**3. a.** It's two forty-five.

   **b.** It's a quarter to two.

**4. a.** It's noon.

   **b.** It's twelve-thirty.

## ❷ Unscramble the conversation.

*Put the conversation in the correct order.*

| | |
|---|---|
| __1__ | Hello? |
| _____ | *Fatal Love.* Do you want to go? |
| _____ | Great! Bye! |
| _____ | Hi, Monica. This is Anna. |
| _____ | Really? What is it? |
| _____ | OK. See you there at a quarter after seven. |
| _____ | Oh, hi, Anna! How are you? |
| _____ | Maybe. What time? |
| _____ | I'm fine. Listen. There's a good movie at the Roxie tonight. |
| _____ | It's at seven-thirty. |
| _____ | Bye! |

## ③ Write answers.

*Look at the calendar pages.*

**WEDNESDAY JULY 7**
6 pm meeting at school

**THURSDAY JULY 8**
8 pm movie Roxie Theater

**FRIDAY JULY 9**
7:30 play Palace Theater

**SATURDAY JULY 10**
2:30 rock concert at the park

**SUNDAY JULY 11**
3:00 baseball game on TV

*Answer the questions.*

1. Where is the meeting? _____It's at school._____

2. What time is the meeting? _____It's at 6:00._____

3. What time is the movie? _____

4. Where is the movie? _____

5. What time is the rock concert? _____

6. Where is the play? _____

7. What time is the baseball game? _____

8. What time is the play? _____

9. Where is the rock concert? _____

## ④ Complete the sentences.

*Fill in the blanks with* is *or* **are**.

1. There _____is_____ a good movie on TV tonight.

2. There _____are_____ three girls in my family.

3. There _____ twenty computers in the school.

4. There _____ a burglar in the house.

5. There _____ water on the table.

6. There _____ a good play at the theater.

7. There _____ three bedrooms in the house.

8. There _____ milk in the glass.

9. There _____ rice for dinner tonight.

## 5 Match questions and answers.

*Match the questions with the answers.*

1. __d__      What movie is at the Lido tonight?     **a.** I'm fine.

2. _____      I'm Allen. What's your name?     **b.** It's ten to seven.

3. _____      Are you married?     **c.** It's at the Palace Theater.

4. _____      Is he married?     **d.** *Fatal Love.*

5. _____      What time is it?     **e.** I'm Paul, and this is Cindy.

6. _____      Where's the concert?     **f.** Yes, I am.

7. _____      How are you?     **g.** No, he isn't. He's single.

## 6 Rewrite a message.

*Write the message with correct punctuation.*

hi julie
how are you theres a great movie at the roxie its called *true love* its at six oclock do you
want to go with me
sara

# 7 Read and answer questions.

**A.** Look at the advertisement for a movie. Answer the questions. Use short answers.

| Questions | Answers |
|---|---|
| **1.** What movie is it? | Loving You. |
| **2.** What time is the movie? | |
| **3.** Who's in the movie? | |
| **4.** Where is the movie? | |

**B.** Now write your own questions about this movie.

| Questions | Answers |
|---|---|
| **1.** _____? | *Escape from Philadelphia.* |
| **2.** _____? | Kurt Costner. |
| **3.** _____? | At the Galaxy Theater. |
| **4.** _____? | At 1:10, 4:30, and 7:50. |

# 8 Write sentences.

**A.** *Circle the things that you see in the picture.*

supermarkets      (water)          trees          restaurants

a theater          a museum      a zoo         an airport

a university       schools         houses

**Challenge**

**B.** *Now write sentences about the picture. Use **there is** and **there are**.*

**Example:** _There is a museum in the picture._

1. _____

2. _____

3. _____

4. _____

5. _____

# For computer questions, press one now.

**1 Identify the speaker.**

*Who is speaking? Write **teacher**, **mother**, or **friend**.*

**teacher**

**mother**

**friend**

"Open your books to page 47."

1.      teacher

"Don't be late for dinner."

2. _____

"Please help me with my homework."

3. _____

"Do page 24 for homework."

4. _____

"Be home at 11:00 P.M.!"

5. _____

"Don't tell my mother!"

6. _____

## ❷ Match beginnings and endings.

*Find the second part of each sentence. Write the correct letter in the blank.*

1. __b__     We're not at home. Please leave     **a.** late.

2. _____     Jeannie, call     **b.** a message.

3. _____     Do you want to go     **c.** a video tonight.

4. _____     Do you have a problem? Talk     **d.** for a walk?

5. _____     Let's watch     **e.** to the teacher.

6. _____     Don't hang     **f.** your mother.

7. _____     Don't be     **g.** up! Stay on the line.

## ❸ Complete the conversation.

*Fill in the blanks in the conversation. Use **Let's** or **Do you want to**.*

**A:** _Do you want to_ go out tonight?
         **1.**

**B:** Good idea. How about a movie?

**A:** OK. _____ go to the Roxie.
         **2.**

**B:** What's playing at the Roxie?

**A:** I don't know. _____ look in the newspaper. . . *Fatal Love.*
         **3.**

_____ see that?
    **4.**

**B:** No, not really. Forget the movie. How about a restaurant? _____ eat out?
         **5.**

**A:** Sure. Where?

**B:** How about Enrico's? It's Italian. It's good.

**A:** OK. _____ walk?
    **6.**

**B:** No, I'm tired. _____ drive instead.
    **7.**

# ❹ Complete the sentences.

*Fill in each blank with a possessive adjective.*

1. Ellen is in _____*her*_____ room.

2. I can't go out now! _____ hair is wet!

3. This is for Tom. _____ birthday is tomorrow.

4. Give me that! That's _____ book!

5. Hello. I'm Patty. What's _____ name?

6. My parents are out tonight. It's _____ wedding anniversary.

7. Today is _____ birthday. I'm six.

8. Hi. I'm Manny, and this is _____ wife, Sylvia.

9. The children are at the movies with _____ friends.

10. What a pretty cat! What's _____ name?

# ❺ Rewrite sentences.

*Rewrite the sentences with the correct punctuation.*

1. its johns birthday on monday

   _It's John's birthday on Monday._

2. marys party is on wednesday

   _____

3. thats mr johnsons house

   _____

4. its my parents anniversary tomorrow

   _____

5. the childrens party is next friday

   _____

## 6 Write sentences.

*Look at the pictures. Write sentences with possessive nouns.*

**David**

**Samantha**

**Alex**

**mug**

**glasses**

**1.** It's Alex's mug.

**2.** They're David's glasses.

**armchair**

**CD player**

**3.** _____

**4.** _____

**T-shirt**

**newspaper**

**5.** _____

**6.** _____

# 7 Complete the puzzle.

*Look at the pictures. Write the correct word or words across each line. What's the extra word?*

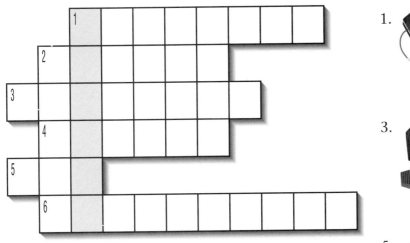

The extra word is _____.

# 8 Write the answers.

*Look at the family tree. Then answer the questions.*

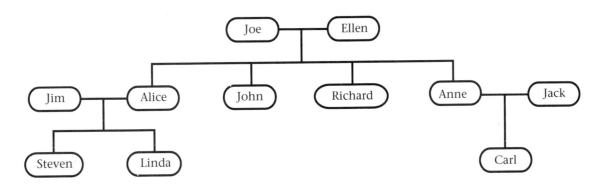

**1.** Who is Joe's wife?  _____ Ellen _____

**2.** Who are Richard's sisters?  __Alice__ and __Anne__

**3.** Who are Ellen's daughters?  _____ and _____

**4.** Who is Linda's grandfather?  _____

**5.** Who are Alice's brothers?  _____ and _____

**6.** Who is Carl's grandmother?  _____

**7.** Who is Alice's son?  _____

# What's Bob doing?

## ❶ Match statements and pictures.

*Look at the pictures. Match each sentence with the correct picture.*

1. ___e___      They're playing ball.

2. _____      He's studying.

3. _____      She's talking to a friend.

4. _____      He's exercising.

5. _____      He's fixing the car.

6. _____      She's watching TV.

a.

b.

c.

d.

e.

f.

## ❷ Complete the sentences.

*Complete each sentence with the correct word from the box. Use some words more than once.*

| playing | doing | going | making | watching |

1. I'm _____doing_____ my homework.

2. We're _____ tennis.

3. I'm _____ dinner.

4. He's _____ for a walk.

5. They're _____ a video.

6. They're _____ baseball.

7. Amy is _____ TV.

8. Mom is _____ pizza.

## ❸ Complete the paragraph.

*Look at the picture. Write the correct form of the verb in the blank.*

It's Saturday afternoon in Bellville. The sun _____is shining_____. The Munson
               **1.** shine

family is at home. Gloria Munson _____ a book. Her son Peter
          **2.** read

and his friend _____ basketball. Alice, her daughter, _____ on
    **3.** play            **4.** talk

the phone. Baby Anne _____. Gloria's husband, Tom, _____ a
      **5.** sleep          **6.** fix

bicycle. Adam, from Sal's Pizza, _____ a pizza. Two people _____
         **7.** deliver         **8.** walk

down the street. The Munson's neighbors _____ their car.
            **9.** wash

## ❹ Write questions.

*Alice is talking to her grandmother in Florida.*
*Read their conversation. Write the questions.*

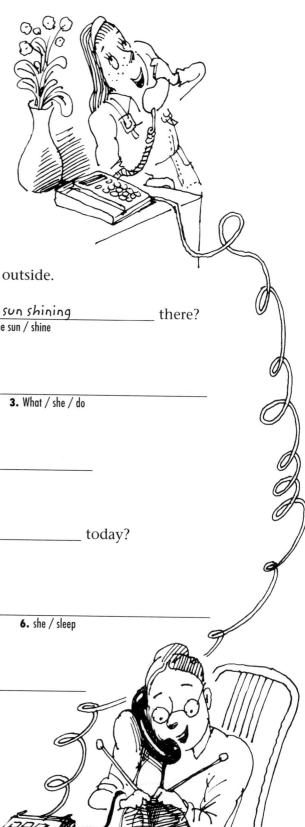

**A:** Grandma? This is Alice.

**B:** Alice! What a nice surprise! Hello, dear.

_____ *What are you doing?* _____
        **1.** What / you / do

**A:** Oh, nothing.

**B:** Where are you?

**A:** I'm at home. I'm inside. But everyone else is outside.

**B:** Outside? It's raining here. _____ *Is the sun shining* _____ there?
                                        **2.** the sun / shine

**A:** Yes, it's a beautiful day.

**B:** And what about your Mom? _____
                                        **3.** What / she / do

**A:** She's reading.

**B:** That's nice. _____
                        **4.** What / she / read

**A:** A new book.

**B:** And your Dad? _____ today?
                        **5.** What / he / do

**A:** He's here. He's fixing his bike.

**B:** That's good. How's the baby? _____
                                        **6.** she / sleep

**A:** Yes, she's sleeping now. She's fine.

**B:** And Peter? _____
                        **7.** What / he / do

**A:** He's with his friend Mario.

**B:** _____
        **8.** What / they / do

**A:** Playing basketball. What about you, Gran?

_____
        **9.** What / you / do

**B:** I'm making a sweater for your baby sister.

# ⑤ Write ordinal numbers.

*Unscramble the words.*

DRITH    _____third_____      TOURFH    _____

THENT    _____      NOSCED    _____

THIFF    _____      THISX    _____

THINN    _____      STIRF    _____

VENSETH    _____      THIGHE    _____

# ⑥ Complete the sentences.

*Write the correct object pronouns in the blanks.*

1. Where's Anne? There's a phone call for _____her_____.

2. John, listen to me! I'm talking to _____!

3. That's my book! Give it to _____!

4. My homework? I'm doing _____ now.

5. Alice and John? We're meeting _____ tonight.

6. My sister's in Kenya. I'm writing a letter to _____ now.

7. We're watching a movie. Come and watch it with _____!

8. That's a good book. We're reading _____ in class.

9. The children are going to the baseball game. Let's go with _____.

10. Anita is at Luigi's Pizza, and Josh is with _____.

11. You're going to New York? Is your wife going with _____?

12. We're lost. Please give _____ directions.

## 7 Write answers.

**A.** Look at the map.

Then answer the questions that follow.

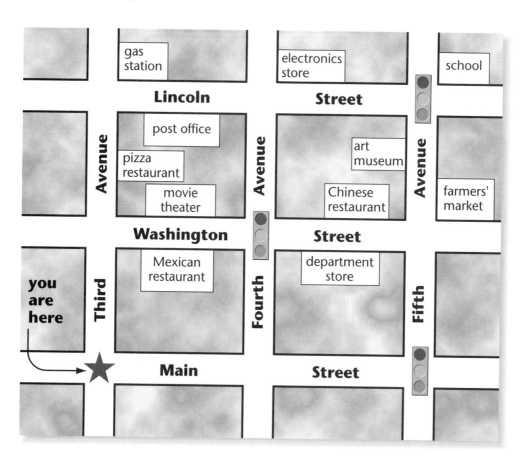

**1.** Where is the electronics store?

   _It's on Lincoln Street, at the corner of Fourth Avenue._

**2.** Where is the gas station?

   _____

**3.** Where is the Mexican restaurant?

   _____

**4.** Where is the Chinese restaurant?

   _____

**5.** Where is the farmers' market?

   _____

*B.* *Now read the directions. Start at* **Main Street and Third Avenue.**

1. Walk down Main Street to Fifth Avenue. Turn left. It's between Washington Street and Lincoln Street, on the left.

   What is it? _____ It's the art museum. _____

2. Go down Third Avenue to Lincoln Street. Turn right. It's between Third Avenue and Fourth Avenue, on the right.

   What is it? _____

3. Go to the corner of Main Street and Fourth Avenue. Turn left on Fourth Avenue. Go one block. Turn right on Washington Street. It's between Fourth Avenue and Fifth Avenue, on the right.

   What is it? _____

4. Walk down Main Street to Fifth Avenue. Turn left on Fifth Avenue. Walk two blocks. It's on the right, on the corner of Lincoln Street and Fifth Avenue.

   What is it? _____

5. Go down Third Avenue to Washington Street. It's on Third Avenue, between Washington Street and Lincoln Street, on the right.

   What is it? _____

## Unit 5  You lose it. We find it.

### ❶ Choose the correct verb.

*Complete the paragraph. Circle the correct form of the verbs.*

Masako and Hiro Hayashi (**1.** (live) / lives) in Tokyo, Japan. Hiro (**2.** work / works) in an electronics company. Masako (**3.** work / works) part-time. They have two daughters, Keiko and Tomiko. The girls (**4.** go / goes) to school five days a week. Keiko also (**5.** go / goes) to school on Saturday mornings.

The Hayashis (**6.** eat / eats) breakfast at 6:30. Hiro (**7.** take / takes) the train to work at 7: 30. The girls (**8.** leave / leaves) for school at 8:00. Then Masako (**9.** do / does) the shopping. Sometimes she (**10.** visit / visits) a neighbor. Then she (**11.** make / makes) dinner for the family. In the evenings, the girls (**12.** do / does) homework and (**13.** watch / watches) TV. Hiro often (**14.** come / comes) home late.

### ❷ Match questions and answers.

**A.** *Match the questions with the answers.*

| | | |
|---|---|---|
| **1.** ___d___ | What's your name? | **a.** No, part-time. I work full-time. |
| **2.** _____ | Do you study full-time? | **b.** Not really. It's a hard job. |
| **3.** _____ | What do you do? | **c.** In Belmont. It's near San Francisco. |
| **4.** _____ | Do you like your job? | **d.** Alex. |
| **5.** _____ | When do you work? | **e.** I'm a taxi driver. |
| **6.** _____ | Where do you live? | **f.** Yes, I have a son. |
| **7.** _____ | Do you have children? | **g.** Five days a week, twelve hours a day. |

**B.** *Now put the words in the correct order to make six questions about Alex. Then answer the questions, using the information on page 22. Use short answers.*

**Questions**        **Answers**

**1.** Alex / do / does / What

     What does Alex do ?                He's a taxi driver.

**2.** Alex / Does / full-time / work

 

**3.** he / does / Where / live

 

**4.** work / When / he / does

 

**5.** have / he / a / Does / daughter

 

**6.** his / he / job / Does / like

 

## ❸ Check the boxes.

**A.** *What do you think about these subjects? Put checks ( ✔ ) in the boxes.*

|  | **Easy** | **Hard** | **Interesting** | **Exciting** | **Boring** |
|---|---|---|---|---|---|
| art |  |  |  |  |  |
| business |  |  |  |  |  |
| computers |  |  |  |  |  |
| dance |  |  |  |  |  |
| journalism |  |  |  |  |  |
| math |  |  |  |  |  |
| medicine |  |  |  |  |  |
| music |  |  |  |  |  |

*(continued on next page)*

***B.*** *Now write five sentences.*

**Example:** I think art is exciting.
• • • • • •

**1.** _____

**2.** _____

**3.** _____

**4.** _____

**5.** _____

## ❹ Write questions.

*Read the sentences. Then write questions to complete the conversation.*

**1. A:** _____Where do you work, Anna_____?

   **B:** I work in the library at City University.

**2. A:** _____ your job?

   **B:** Oh, yes. I love it.

**3. A:** _____ full-time?

   **B:** No, part-time.

**4. A:** _____?

   **B:** I work from ten to two.

**5. A:** _____?

   **B:** I live on 35th Street. It's only five blocks from the university.

## ❺ Write verbs.

*Write the third person singular form of each verb in the simple present tense.*

**1.** look __looks__   **2.** drink _____   **3.** teach _____   **4.** study _____

**5.** love _____   **6.** get _____   **7.** have _____   **8.** do _____

**9.** live _____   **10.** watch _____   **11.** worry _____   **12.** speak _____

# ⑥ Write about Carmen and Anna.

**A.** *Look at the pictures. Fill in the charts.*

**Carmen's house**

**Anna's house**

|  | Carmen | Anna |  | Carmen | Anna |
|---|:---:|:---:|---|:---:|:---:|
| **1.** has a child | ✔ |  | **5.** loves to cook |  |  |
| **2.** studies part-time |  |  | **6.** plays tennis |  |  |
| **3.** has a dog |  |  | **7.** plays guitar |  |  |
| **4.** loves to travel |  |  | **8.** wears glasses |  |  |

**B.** *Now write about Carmen and Anna.*

**Carmen**

Carmen has a child.

_____

_____

_____

**Anna**

Anna studies part-time.

_____

_____

_____

_____

## ❼ Write about yourself.

**A.** *Answer the questions. Tell about yourself.*

> **Example:** Do you study full-time?  ___No, I study part-time.___

1. Where do you live?  _____

2. Do you live in an apartment?  _____

3. Do you live alone?  _____

4. What do you do every morning?  _____

5. What do you eat for breakfast?  _____

6. When do you eat lunch?  _____

7. What do you do in the evenings?  _____

8. Do you exercise?  _____

9. Do you watch TV?  _____

10. Do you like music?  _____

**B.** *A pen pal is a person who lives far away. Pen pals write letters to each other. Write a postcard to a new pen pal. Write about yourself. Use some of the information from above. Sign the letter with your name.*

Dear pen pal,

　　My name is _____ and I live in _____

_____

I_____

_____

_____

_____

_____

　　　　　　　　　Sincerely,

　　　　　　　　　_____

　　　　　　　　　*(Sign your name here.)*

## ❶ Complete the questions.

_Fill in the blanks with **Do, Does, Are,** or **Is.**_

1. _____Do_____ you like your job?

2. _____Is_____ there a concert tonight?

3. _____ it raining?

4. _____ you have a computer?

5. _____ Alex have children?

6. _____ there a post office on Washington Street?

7. _____ you married?

8. _____ they working today?

9. _____ Mario like school?

10. _____ you have grandchildren?

11. _____ there a farmers' market here?

12. _____ Peter work full-time?

## ❷ Match verbs and objects.

_Draw lines from each verb to one or two words in the circle._

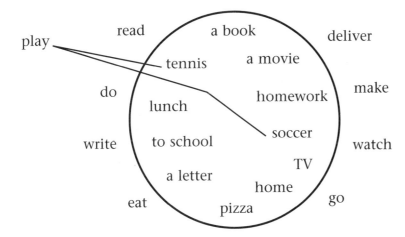

read   a book   deliver

play

tennis   a movie

do   homework   make

lunch

write   to school   soccer   watch

a letter   TV

home

eat   pizza   go

## ❸ Complete the conversation.

*Fill in the blanks with the correct words from the box. Use each word only once.*

| at | ~~from~~ | of | on | to |
|----|----------|-----|-----|-----|

**A:** John? Is that you? Listen. We're lost.

**B:** Well, where are you calling _____*from*_____?
   **1.**

**A:** We're _____ the corner _____ Fifth and Main Street.
   **2.**   **3.**

**B:** OK. Go _____ the light. Turn left. We're the third house _____ the right.
   **4.**   **5.**

**A:** OK. Thanks. See you soon!

## *Challenge* ❹ Test your memory.

*Take five minutes. Write more words in each category. How many do you remember?*

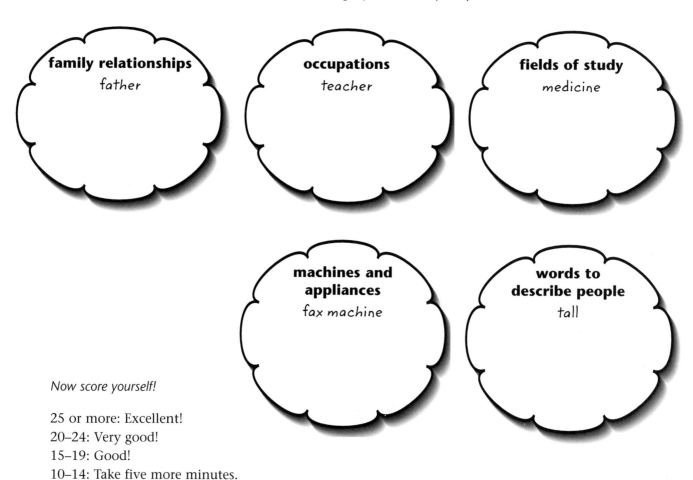

**family relationships**
father

**occupations**
teacher

**fields of study**
medicine

**machines and appliances**
fax machine

**words to describe people**
tall

*Now score yourself!*

25 or more: Excellent!
20–24: Very good!
15–19: Good!
10–14: Take five more minutes.
1–9: Look at Units 1–5 again.

## ⑤ Write the expression.

*Write the correct expression for each picture.*

Let's go to a movie. ~~Sorry I'm late.~~
Nice to meet you. We're lost.

**1.** <u>Sorry I'm late.</u>

**2.** _____

**3.** _____

**4.** _____

## ⑥ Rewrite sentences.

*Rewrite the sentences with the correct punctuation.*

**1.** theres a movie at the roxie on wednesday

  <u>There's a movie at the Roxie on Wednesday.</u>

**2.** he doesnt work on saturdays

  _____

**3.** mrs clark is peters grandmother

  _____

**4.** anna is at marias house

  _____